THE NEW TESTAMENT
SIMPLY EXPLAINED

CHRISTIAN BOULANGER

Copyright © 2023 Christian Boulanger

All rights reserved.

ISBN: 9798870127361

DEDICATION

For my family

CONTENTS

	Foreword	
1	Fundamentals	Page 1
2	Mary and Joseph	Page 3
3	The 3 kings	Page 5
4	The stable	Page 7
5	The evening star	Page 9
6	The virgin birth	Page 11
7	Jesus the carpenter	Page 12
8	Jesus became Christ	Page 14
9	The hike through the desert	Page 15
10	The baptism by John	Page 17
11	John's imprisonment	Page 18
12	Jesus and his	Page 19

	disciples	
13	The wonders	Page 21
14	The Sermon on the Mount	Page 23
15	Symbolic consideration	Page 25
16	Mary Magdalene	Page 28
17	The Last Supper	Page 29
18	How does Leonardo da Vinci see the Last Supper?	Page 31
19	Judas	Page 32
20	Before the cock crows three times	Page 33
21	How old was Jesus?	Page 35
22	The crucifixion	Page 36
23	The robe	Page 37
24	The crown of thorns	Page 39
25	The crucifixion and dissolution of hereditary guilt	Page 41
26	The spear	Page 44

27	Burial and resurrection	Page 45
28	Why are there different gospels?	Page 49
29	Gospel of Thomas	Page 51
30	New Gospels	Page 53
31	The Revelation of John	Page 54
32	Meaning of the revelation	Page 56
33	The Lamb of God	Page 58
34	Bearing the sin of the world	Page 60
35	The Seven Seals	Page 61
36	The Trinity	Page 62
37	The Holy Grail	Page 64
38	Jesus as Savior	Page 66
39	The archangel	Page 68
40	Satan and the devil	Page 69
41	Satan outside the New Testament	Page 71
42	Pontius Pilate	Page 73

43	Herod	Page 75
44	Salome	Page 77
45	Christian holidays	Page 79
46	The shroud	Page 89
47	Jesus vs. Osiris	Page 83
48	Jesus and Buddha	Page 85
49	Jesus and Islam	Page 86
50	Jesus and Judaism	Page 87
51	Jesus and the Rosenkreutzer	Page 89
52	Differences in beliefs	Page 90
53	Orthodox Church	Page 92
54	Gnosis	Page 94
55	New age movement	Page 95
56	Buddhism and Hinduism	Page 97
57	Taoism	Page 99
58	Judaism	Page 100
59	Islam	Page 102
60	Freemasonry	Page 103

61	Shamatism	Page 105
62	The importance of religion and faith	Page 106
63	What significance does God have for humanity?	Page 108
64	The meaning of life	Page 110
65	Life after death	Page 112
66	The Omega Point	Page 113
67	Parraleluniverses	Page 114
68	Akasha	Page 115

Foreword

The New Testament is an important part of the Bible and, through the Gospels, contains the stories and messages of Jesus Christ and his disciples. It is rich in symbolism, representing different aspects of faith and spiritual teachings.

The greatest story of mankind is not considered credible by today's intellect. In this book, we want to read between the lines and decipher the symbolism of the New Testament. The result will astonish many, because it will awaken a completely new way of looking at things. Immerse yourself in the deepest secrets of the symbolism of the New Testament that has remained hidden for too long.

CHAPTER 1

Basic symbols and terms

Cross

The cross is the central symbol of Christianity and represents the sacrificial death of Jesus Christ for the redemption of mankind. It also symbolizes the love of God and victory over sin and death.

Baptism

Baptism is a sacrament in Christianity that symbolizes the cleansing of sins and acceptance into the community of believers. It stands for the beginning of a new life in faith.

Bread and wine

In the Lord's Supper, bread and wine symbolize the body and blood of Jesus Christ. They are a reminder of his sacrifice on the cross and stand for communion, renewal and spiritual nourishment.

Light

Light is often used as a symbol for truth, knowledge, revelation and divine presence. Jesus is often referred to as the "light of the world" in the New Testament.

Shepherd

Jesus is often depicted as a shepherd who leads, protects and cares for his sheep. This symbol stands for care, guidance and love.

Fish

The fish was an early symbol of Christianity and was used by the first Christians to show their faith. It stands for Jesus Christ as the "fisher of men" and also symbolizes community and unity.

Resurrection

The resurrection of Jesus Christ symbolizes the victory over death and the hope of eternal life. It is a central theme in the New Testament and stands for redemption and rebirth.

Symbols in the New Testament are not only to be understood literally, but also metaphorically and spiritually. They serve to convey deep spiritual truths and strengthen faith.

CHAPTER 2

Mary and Joseph

Mary and Joseph are two central figures in the Christian tradition, particularly in connection with the birth of Jesus Christ. They have a symbolic meaning that represents various aspects of faith and human experience.

Mary as mother: Mary is depicted as the mother of Jesus and symbolizes motherhood itself. Her willingness to conceive and bear the child of God shows her devotion and obedience to God. Mary is often referred to as the "new Eve", as she plays a decisive role in the redemption of humanity. She represents the unconditional love of a mother and embodies the ideals of care, protection and charity.

Joseph as father: Joseph is depicted as Mary's husband and Jesus' stepfather. He symbolizes fatherhood and represents virtues such as responsibility, protection and leadership. Joseph accepts Jesus as his own child, although he is not biologically related to him. This shows his willingness to take responsibility and stand up for the welfare of others. Joseph also stands for obedience to God's will and his role as protector of the Holy Family.

Humility and obedience: Both Mary and Joseph are often praised for their humility and obedience to God's plan. They accept their roles in the story of redemption without reservation or doubt. Their willingness to follow God's will symbolizes the importance of humility and obedience in the Christian faith. They serve as role models for believers who should also be willing to accept and obey God's will.

Human experience: Mary and Joseph were normal people

with their own fears, doubts and challenges. Their journey to Bethlehem, their search for shelter and their birth in a stable show the human experience of difficulties and hardship. Through their experiences, they become symbols of human suffering and the hope of redemption. They remind us that God is present in the midst of our human weakness and need.

The symbolic significance of Mary and Joseph therefore lies in their role as Jesus' parents, their virtues such as humility and obedience, their human experience of suffering and hope and their function as role models for believers. They embody important aspects of the Christian faith and serve as inspiration for a life in harmony with God's will.

CHAPTER 3

The three kings

The Magi, also known as the Wise Men from the East or the Magi, are figures from the biblical story of the birth of Jesus Christ. They have a symbolic meaning that represents various aspects of faith and the human search for God.

Representation of peoples: The Three Wise Men are often depicted as representatives of different peoples and cultures. Traditionally, they are referred to as Caspar, Melchior and Balthasar and come from the East, which indicates their origin from different countries. This depiction symbolizes the universal significance of the birth of Jesus Christ for all people, regardless of their origin or culture.

Search for truth: The Magi traveled great distances to find the newborn Jesus. Their search symbolizes the human longing for truth and spiritual fulfillment. They were prepared to leave their comfort zone and overcome obstacles to find the child they believed to be the promised Messiah. Their search represents man's inner urge for meaning and orientation in his life.

Adoration and devotion: When the Magi found the child Jesus, they prostrated themselves before him and offered him gifts. These actions symbolize worship and devotion to God. The gifts - gold, frankincense and myrrh - also have symbolic meanings. Gold stands for royalty and wealth, frankincense for divine worship and myrrh for sacrifice and suffering. Through their worship, the Magi show their recognition of Jesus' divine nature and their willingness to dedicate their lives to him.

Revelation of Messiahship: The arrival of the Magi to Jesus was seen as a revelation of Jesus' Messiahship. Their presence and gifts confirmed the prophecies about the coming Messiah. This also had political implications, as it pointed to the universal reign of Jesus and emphasized his importance for all peoples.

The symbolic significance of the Magi therefore lies in their representation of the nations, their search for truth, their worship and devotion to God and their role in revealing the Messiahship of Jesus. They remind us that the message of Jesus Christ is for all people and that through our search for God and our devotion to him, we can find a deeper connection to him.

CHAPTER 4

The stable

Humility and modesty: The stable was a simple and modest place for the birth of Jesus. It was not a magnificent or royal setting, but a place for animals. This depiction symbolizes the humility and modesty of Jesus, who came to earth as the Son of God to be close to people. The stable reminds us that God does not reveal himself in power and wealth, but in simplicity and lowliness.

Connection to creation: The stable as a place for animals also shows a close connection to creation. Jesus was born in the midst of animals, which points to his role as the redeemer of all creation. This depiction emphasizes the importance of environmental protection and man's responsibility towards nature.

Fulfillment of biblical prophecies: The birth of Jesus in the stable also fulfills biblical prophecies. Micah 5:1 reads: "And you, Bethlehem, in the land of Judah, are by no means least among the princes of Judah; for out of you shall come to me the duke who is to be ruler over my people Israel." Bethlehem was the place where Jesus was born, and the stable was part of this fulfillment of prophecy.

Invitation to accept: The stable also symbolizes an invitation to accept Jesus Christ. The stable was the only place available for Mary and Joseph to give birth to their child. This depiction reminds us that Jesus came into the world to be accepted by people, regardless of their social status or background. The stable is a symbol of God's openness to all people and his invitation to acceptance and relationship.

Contrast with royal expectations: Jesus' birth in the stable also contrasts with the royal expectations of the time. Many Jews expected a powerful and magnificent Messiah who would wield political power. However, Jesus' birth in the stable shows that his kingship is different - it is based on love, humility and service to others.

The symbolic meaning of the stable in the Christmas story thus emphasizes the humility and modesty of Jesus, his connection to creation, the fulfillment of biblical prophecy, the invitation to acceptance and the contrast to the worldly idea of royalty. The stable reminds us that God is present in the midst of our simplest and most humble circumstances and that we can welcome Jesus into our lives, regardless of external circumstances or expectations.

CHAPTER 5

The evening star

The evening star, also known as the planet Venus, has a symbolic meaning in various cultures and traditions. Here are some possible interpretations:

Light and guidance: The evening star is one of the brightest objects in the night sky and can therefore serve as a symbol of light and guidance. At night, it serves as a point of orientation and helps people to find their way. This symbolic meaning can be applied on a spiritual level by viewing the evening star as a symbol of divine guidance and enlightenment.

Beauty and love: The evening star is often associated with beauty and love. In mythology, the goddess Venus was associated with the planet Venus and was considered the goddess of love, beauty and fertility. The evening star can therefore be seen as a symbol of romantic love, attraction and aesthetic beauty.

Duality: The evening star appears both in the morning and evening sky, depending on whether it is visible before or after sunrise. This duality can be symbolic of opposites, such as day and night, light and darkness or life and death. The evening star reminds us that life is made up of different aspects and that it is important to find a balance between them.

Hope: The evening star can also be seen as a symbol of hope. When darkness falls and the stars appear in the sky, the evening star can serve as a sign of light and hope in the midst of darkness. It reminds us that there is always a spark of hope, even in the most difficult times.

Transcendence: The evening star that appears in the sky can

also be seen as a symbol of the transcendent. In many cultures, the sky is seen as a place of the divine, and the evening star can point to the connection between the earthly and the heavenly. It reminds us that there is a greater reality that transcends our earthly existence.

The symbolic meaning of the evening star can vary depending on the cultural context and individual interpretation. Overall, however, it often represents light, guidance, beauty, love, duality, hope and transcendence. The evening star reminds us that there is more than what is visible and that we can connect with the divine to find guidance and inspiration.

CHAPTER 6

The virgin birth

The virgin birth is a central dogma of faith in Christianity, which states that Jesus Christ was conceived by the Holy Spirit in the Virgin Mary without the involvement of a human father. This event is described in the New Testament and has great theological significance. Here are some possible interpretations of the virgin birth:

Fulfillment of biblical prophecies: The virgin birth is often seen as a fulfillment of Old Testament prophecies, especially Isaiah 7:14: "Behold, a virgin shall be with child and bear a son." This is interpreted as a sign of the coming of the Messiah.

Divine intervention: The virgin birth is seen as a divine miracle in which God himself intervenes in the world and conceives Jesus in an extraordinary way. It shows the uniqueness and divinity of Jesus Christ.

Purity and sinlessness: The virgin birth is sometimes associated with the idea that Mary remained a virgin before and after the birth of Jesus. This symbolizes her purity and sinlessness and ensures that Jesus is free from original sin.

Incarnation of God: The virgin birth emphasizes the incarnation of God in Jesus Christ. Through his birth from a woman, he shows his connection to human nature and can thus be a perfect sacrifice for the sins of mankind.

It is important to note that the virgin birth is a dogma of faith and cannot be scientifically proven. It is interpreted and emphasized differently by different Christian traditions. For believers, it symbolizes the uniqueness and divinity of Jesus Christ and his role as redeemer and savior of mankind.

CHAPTER 7

Jesus of Nazareth the carpenter

Jesus of Nazareth, the carpenter, has a profound meaning and symbolism that represents various aspects of his life and teachings.

Humility and simplicity: The fact that Jesus worked as a carpenter symbolizes his humility and simplicity. As the Son of God, he could have chosen any position or vocation, but he chose to practice a simple trade. This depiction emphasizes the importance of humility and service in following Jesus.

Human experience: Through his work as a carpenter, Jesus was able to fully understand and share the human experience. He knew first-hand the challenges and difficulties of daily life. This symbolism emphasizes Jesus' humanity and his ability to identify with people.

Creative power: As a carpenter, Jesus was also a creator. He was able to create and design

something new from simple materials. This symbolism points to the divine creative power that was at work in Jesus. It reminds us that God is not only the creator of the universe, but is also able to reshape and transform our lives.

Work ethic: The fact that Jesus worked as a carpenter also shows his work ethic and commitment to hard work. His work was not only a means of earning a living, but also a way of putting his faith into practice and serving others. This symbolism emphasizes the importance of diligence, commitment and dedication in our own lives.

Community and cooperation: As a carpenter, Jesus probably

worked in close community with other craftsmen. This symbolism emphasizes the importance of community and cooperation in our life of faith. It reminds us that as Christians we are called to work together and support each other to build the kingdom of God.

The symbolic meaning of Jesus as a carpenter therefore lies in his humility and simplicity, his ability to share the human experience, his creative power, his work ethic and his commitment to community and cooperation. This symbolism encourages us to follow Jesus' example and use our talents and abilities in service to God and mankind.

CHAPTER 8

Jesus became Christ

The term "Christ" is a Greek translation of the Hebrew word "Messiah", which means "the anointed one". In the Christian faith, Jesus of Nazareth is regarded as the Christ or the Messiah.

The significance of Jesus as Christ lies in the fact that, according to the faith of Christians, he fulfilled the promises and prophecies of the Old Testament. In the Old Testament, various prophecies were made about a coming redeemer who would save the people of Israel and redeem the world. Christians believe that Jesus fulfilled this role.

Jesus was seen as the Christ because he:

Fulfilled the promises of the Old Testament: Jesus fulfilled numerous prophecies about the Messiah, including his birth from a virgin (Isaiah 7:14), his descent from King David (2 Samuel 7:12-13) and his birth in Bethlehem (Micah 5:1).

The kingdom of God proclaimed: Jesus preached about a kingdom of God that was near and in which God would establish his reign. He taught about love, forgiveness and justice and called on people to convert and follow him.

Performed miracles: Jesus performed numerous miracles, such as healing illnesses, freeing demons and even raising people from the dead. These miracles were seen as signs of his divine power and authority.

Sacrificed his life: Jesus gave his life on the cross as an atoning sacrifice for the sins of mankind. Christians believe that his death and resurrection opened the way to redemption and reconciliation with God.

The term "Jesus Christ" therefore emphasizes both the name of Jesus and his role as the expected Messiah or anointed one of God. For Christians, Jesus Christ is the central point of their faith and their hope for salvation and eternal life.

CHAPTER 9

The hike through the desert

According to the Gospels, after his baptism in the Jordan River, Jesus went into the desert, where he fasted for forty days and nights and was tempted by Satan.

The meaning of Jesus' wandering through the desert can be interpreted in different ways:

Preparation for his ministry: The time in the desert is often seen as a time of preparation for Jesus' public ministry. Through fasting and temptations, Jesus was prepared for his mission and strengthened his relationship with God.

Overcoming temptation: During his stay in the desert, Jesus was tempted by Satan, who offered him power, fame and worldly domination. Jesus resisted these temptations and showed his devotion to God and his rejection of worldly temptations.

Identification with the people of Israel:

Jesus' wandering through the desert is sometimes seen as a parallel to the wandering of the people of Israel through the desert in the Old Testament. Like the people of Israel, Jesus also had to overcome trials and temptations in order to keep his faith.

Spiritual cleansing and renewal:

The time in the desert can also be seen as a time of spiritual cleansing and renewal. Through fasting and seclusion, Jesus was able to focus on God, deepen his relationship with him and prepare himself for his mission.

Jesus' wandering through the desert is a significant event in the life of Jesus and is often seen as an example of perseverance, dedication and victory over temptation. It also symbolizes the human experience of trials and challenges on the spiritual path.

CHAPTER 10

The baptism by John

The baptism by John the Baptist is an important event in Jesus' life that is described in the New Testament. According to the Gospels, Jesus came to John at the Jordan River to be baptized by him.

The meaning of John's baptism can be interpreted in various ways:

Symbolic cleansing: Baptism by John symbolized a ritual cleansing of sins and a conversion to faith. By being baptized, Jesus showed his willingness to turn away from his sins and embark on a new path.

Identification with the people: Through his baptism, Jesus identified with the people of Israel and their longing for forgiveness and redemption. He placed himself in the ranks of those who hoped in God and looked out for a Messiah.

Confirmation of the mission: John's baptism also served as confirmation of Jesus' mission and calling. After the baptism, heaven was opened, the Holy Spirit descended on Jesus and a voice from heaven proclaimed: "This is my beloved Son, in whom I am well pleased." This confirmed Jesus in his path as the Messiah and gave him divine authority.

Example of discipleship: Jesus' baptism can also be seen as an example of following Christ. By being baptized, Jesus shows believers the way to repentance, acceptance of faith and devotion to God.

The baptism by John marks the beginning of Jesus' public ministry and symbolizes his devotion to God and his willingness to take upon himself the sins of mankind. It is a significant event in the life of Jesus and has important theological significance for the understanding of the Christian faith.

CHAPTER 11

John's imprisonment

The imprisonment of John the Baptist is another event described in the New Testament. After John baptized Jesus, he came into conflict with Herod Antipas, the ruler of Galilee and Perea. John publicly criticized Herod's unlawful marriage to Herodias, his brother's wife.

The meaning of John's imprisonment can be interpreted in various ways:

Witness to the truth: John's imprisonment shows his determination to proclaim the truth and stand up against injustice. Despite the possible consequences for his own life, he remained steadfast in his faith and his proclamation.

Sacrifice for the faith: John's imprisonment also shows the willingness of a believer to suffer and even sacrifice his life for his faith. John was eventually beheaded on Herod's orders because he refused to retract his criticism.

Prophetic tradition: John's imprisonment and execution are reminiscent of the similar fates of other biblical prophets such as Jeremiah or Elijah. This underlines the continuity of the prophetic tradition in Judaism and shows that the word of God often encounters resistance.

Harbinger of Jesus' suffering: John's imprisonment and execution can also be seen as a foreshadowing of Jesus' suffering. Like John, Jesus was also rejected by the religious and political authorities of his time and was ultimately executed.

The imprisonment of John the Baptist is a tragic event that shows the consequences of standing up against injustice and sin.

It reminds believers to remain steadfast in their faith and to be prepared to stand up for the truth, even if this entails personal sacrifice.

CHAPTER 12

Jesus and his disciples

Jesus chose twelve men to be his closest companions and disciples, who became known as his disciples.

The disciples of Jesus were:

Simon Peter: He was one of the first disciples Jesus called and was often regarded as the spokesman for the group.

Andrew: He was Peter's brother and was also called by Jesus at an early stage.

James, son of Zebedee: He was one of the so-called "sons of thunder" and was one of Jesus' closest confidants.

John: He was the brother of James and is often referred to as "the disciple whom Jesus loved".

Philip: He was called by Jesus and played an important role in spreading the gospel.

Bartholomew: Also known as Nathanael, he was another disciple of Jesus.

Matthew: A former tax collector who was called by Jesus and later wrote the Gospel according to Matthew.

Thomas: Known as the "doubter" because he initially doubted the resurrection of Jesus.

James, son of Alphaeus: Also known as James the Younger or James the Just.

Thaddeus: Also known as Lebbaeus or Judas (not Iscariot), to distinguish him from Judas Iscariot.

Simon the Zealot: He is often regarded as a political activist and was part of a Jewish resistance movement against Roman rule.

Judas Iscariot: He was one of Jesus' disciples who would later betray him and hand him over to the Roman authorities.

The disciples of Jesus accompanied him during his ministry, heard his teachings, saw his miracles and were trained by him. They witnessed his crucifixion, resurrection and ascension. After Jesus ascended to heaven, the disciples played a crucial role in spreading the gospel and founding the early Christian communities.

The disciples of Jesus are an example of dedication, faithfulness and the call to proclaim the gospel. Their stories serve as inspiration for Christians to follow their faith and take the word of God into the world.

CHAPTER 13

The miracles that Jesus performed

The symbolic significance of Jesus' miracles lies in the fact that they go beyond their literal meaning and convey profound spiritual teachings. Here are some examples:

Water into wine: This miracle symbolizes the fullness and joy of the kingdom of God. It shows that Jesus is able to transform the ordinary into something extraordinary and fill us with his grace and joy.

Healing of diseases: Jesus' healings symbolize his power over suffering and illness. They show that he can not only bring physical healing, but also spiritual healing and redemption from sin and pain.

Calming the storm: This miracle illustrates Jesus' authority over the forces of nature and symbolizes his peace, which can be found even in the midst of the storm. It reminds us that we can rely on him to protect and guide us in difficult times.

Multiplication of bread: This miracle symbolizes Jesus' provision for our spiritual needs. He is able to multiply the little we have and provide us with his love, wisdom and nourishment for our souls.

Raising Lazarus: The resurrection of Lazarus symbolizes Jesus' power over death and gives a foretaste of his own resurrection. It reminds us that Jesus brings eternal life and that death does not have the last word.

The symbolic meaning of Jesus' miracles is that they help us to delve deeper into faith and to recognize the divine power and love of Jesus. They encourage us to believe in him, trust him and follow him, as he is able to fulfill our needs and gift us with his peace and salvation

CHAPTER 14

The Sermon on the Mount

The Sermon on the Mount is one of Jesus' best-known and most influential speeches, which can be found in the New Testament in the Gospel of Matthew (chapters 5-7). It contains a wealth of teachings and instructions that Jesus gave to his disciples and the crowds. Here are some of the main themes and teachings contained in the Sermon on the Mount:

The Beatitudes: Jesus begins the Sermon on the Mount with the Beatitudes, in which he blesses those who are poor in spirit, mourn, are meek, hunger and thirst for righteousness, are merciful, are pure in heart, are peacemakers and are persecuted for righteousness' sake. These beatitudes show the values of the kingdom of God and encourage us to be humble, merciful and peaceable.

The law and fulfillment: Jesus explains that he did not come to abolish the law, but to fulfill it. However, he also emphasizes the importance of the heart behind outward actions and calls on his disciples to go beyond the commandment and have an inner attitude of love and forgiveness.

The ethics of the kingdom of God: Jesus teaches his disciples various ethical principles such as love of neighbor, love of enemies, forgiveness, honesty and chastity. He calls on them to be righteous not only outwardly, but also in their hearts and motives.

Prayer: Jesus teaches the Lord's Prayer, a model prayer that emphasizes our relationship with God and teaches us to ask for God's kingdom and His will.

Worry and trust: Jesus encourages his disciples not to worry excessively about material things, but to put their trust in God and focus on the kingdom of God.

Judging and condemning: Jesus warns against condemning others and calls on his disciples to act with mercy and forgiveness.

The Sermon on the Mount is a comprehensive guide to living according to the principles of the Kingdom of God. It calls us to be humble, merciful, peaceful and just and to cultivate a deep relationship with God. The teachings of the Sermon on the Mount have had a great influence on Christian ethics and still encourage Christians today to put these values into practice in their daily lives.

CHAPTER 15

The symbolic meaning of the Sermon on the Mount

The Sermon on the Mount contains various symbolic elements that convey deep spiritual meanings. Here are some examples:

The place: The fact that Jesus gave the Sermon on the Mount on a mountain has symbolic significance. Mountains are often seen as places of closeness to God and symbolize majesty, strength and transcendence. By delivering the sermon on a mountain, Jesus emphasized his divine authority and showed that his teachings were of the highest importance.

The Beatitudes: The Beatitudes are a series of statements in which Jesus blesses certain groups of people. They have a symbolic meaning, as they are not only a description of the present condition, but also a promise for the future kingdom of God. They show that true happiness does not lie in external circumstances or material wealth, but in a relationship with God and living according to his principles.

The light of the world and the salt of the earth: Jesus uses these metaphors to describe the role of his disciples in the world. The light stands for truth, knowledge and revelation, while the salt stands for flavor, preservation and purification. These symbols illustrate the disciples' task of proclaiming the gospel and exerting a positive influence on the world through their lives.

The Lord's Prayer: The Lord's Prayer is a model prayer that Jesus taught his disciples. It contains symbolic elements such as the adoration of God as Father, the petition for the coming of the kingdom of God and the request for daily bread. These symbols convey deep spiritual truths about our relationship with God and our dependence on him.

The symbolism in the Sermon on the Mount serves to introduce us deeper into the faith and encourage us to live according to the principles of the Kingdom of God. It reminds us that our lives have spiritual significance and that we are called to be light and salt in the world. The symbolism also helps us to better understand the teachings of Jesus and apply them to our daily lives.

The disciples of Jesus have a symbolic meaning that goes beyond their literal identity. Here are some aspects of their symbolism:

Representatives of the people: The disciples were chosen from different social backgrounds, including fishermen, tax collectors and ordinary workers. They represent the people of Israel and show that Jesus came to redeem all people, regardless of their social status or background.

Disciple and follower: The term "disciple" literally means "pupil" or "follower". The disciples of Jesus symbolize those who are willing to follow him, learn from him and follow his example. They stand for those who decide to acknowledge Jesus as their Lord and seek his kingdom.

Witnesses of the resurrection: The disciples were eyewitnesses of Jesus' resurrection and were commissioned to take his message to the world. They symbolize those who are to proclaim the gospel and bear witness to salvation through Jesus Christ.

Representatives of the church: The disciples are often regarded as the forerunners of the Christian church. They symbolize the community of believers and stand for those who gather around the faith in Jesus Christ and serve God together.

Weakness and transformation: The disciples were not perfect and made mistakes, but they were called by Jesus and transformed by his teachings and example. Their symbolism illustrates that God chooses the weak to proclaim his message and that he is able to change people and empower them for his service.

The symbolism of Jesus' disciples shows us that we are all

called to follow him, to learn from him and to seek his kingdom. It encourages us to be witnesses of his resurrection and to take the gospel into the world. The disciples also symbolize the community of believers and remind us that we are part of the Church of Jesus Christ.

CHAPTER 16

Mary Magdalene

Mary Magdalene plays a significant role in the New Testament and has a symbolic meaning that goes beyond her literal identity. Here are some aspects of her role and symbolism:

A faithful disciple: Mary Magdalene is portrayed as one of Jesus' most faithful disciples. She accompanied Jesus during his ministry and witnessed his crucifixion and burial. Her faithfulness symbolizes the devotion and love for Jesus that we as believers should imitate.

A witness to the resurrection: Mary Magdalene was the first person to meet Jesus after his resurrection. She was commissioned by Jesus to tell the other disciples about his resurrection. Her role as a witness to the resurrection symbolizes the importance of witnessing and proclaiming the gospel.

A symbolic figure for forgiveness and transformation: In some traditions, Mary Magdalene is identified with a sinful woman who was forgiven by Jesus (Luke 7:36-50). This identification symbolizes the message of forgiveness and transformation through Jesus Christ. Mary Magdalene stands for the possibility of repentance and new beginnings, regardless of our past or our mistakes.

A female voice in a male-dominated environment: Mary Magdalene is an important female figure in the New Testament and stands for the importance of women in the ministry of Jesus. She shows that women have an active role in the kingdom of God and that their voices and contributions are valuable.

The role of Mary Magdalene reminds us that as disciples of

Jesus, we are called to follow him faithfully and carry his witness into the world. Her story symbolizes forgiveness, transformation and the importance of the female voice in God's service.

CHAPTER 17

The Last Supper

The Last Supper, which Jesus celebrated with his disciples before his death, has great significance and is rich in symbolism. Here are some aspects of the meaning and symbolism of the Last Supper:

Sacrifice and redemption: The bread and wine used during communion symbolize the body and blood of Jesus Christ. They are a reminder of his imminent sacrifice on the cross to redeem mankind from sin and death. The Last Supper emphasizes the central importance of Jesus' sacrifice for our salvation.

Communion and unity: Eating together at communion symbolizes the fellowship of believers with Christ and with each other. It reminds us that as Christians we are part of a larger community and that we are one through faith in Jesus Christ.

Remembrance and gratitude: The Last Supper also serves as a reminder of the life, ministry and sacrifice of Jesus. It reminds us of how Jesus laid down his life for us and calls us to be grateful for his grace.

Promise of the coming kingdom: Jesus said at the Last Supper that he would only drink the wine again in the kingdom of God (Luke 22:18). This statement symbolizes the hope of the future kingdom of God, in which we will be in perfect communion with God.

Invitation to participate: The Last Supper is an invitation to all believers to participate in communion with Christ. It reminds us that through faith in Jesus Christ we can enter into communion with him and receive his grace.

The meaning and symbolism of the Last Supper remind us of the central event of the Christian faith - the death and resurrection of Jesus Christ. It calls us to gratitude, to communion with Christ and to hope for the coming kingdom of God.

CHAPTER 18

How does Leonardo da Vinci see the Last Supper?

Leonardo da Vinci, one of the greatest artists of the Renaissance, depicted the Last Supper in a famous painting. His interpretation of the Last Supper is known for its artistic brilliance and unique depiction of the figures.

In Leonardo's painting, Jesus and his disciples are arranged at a long table, with Jesus sitting in the middle. The figures are lifelike and show a variety of emotions and reactions to Jesus' words. Leonardo has managed to capture the individual personalities and characters of the disciples.

A notable feature of Leonardo's depiction is the use of perspective and space. He used the technique of central perspective to expand the space and create depth. This draws the viewer into the painting and makes them feel part of the action.

Leonardo also placed great emphasis on details, such as the gestures and expressions of the disciples. Each figure has a unique posture or facial expression that shows their individual reaction to Jesus' words. These details give the painting an emotional depth and make it a captivating work of art.

Leonardo also added symbolic elements to his painting. For example, the window in the background forms a halo around Jesus, which could indicate his divine nature. The arrangement of the disciples in groups of three possibly symbolizes the Trinity.

Leonardo's depiction of the Last Supper is a masterpiece of art history. It not only depicts the biblical event itself, but also captures the emotions, personalities and symbolism of the disciples. The painting is a timeless work that is still admired today and makes a significant contribution to the history of art.

CHAPTER 19

Judas

Judas and the denial are two separate events related to the Last Supper and the Passion of Christ. Here is an explanation of both:

Judas: Judas Iscariot was one of Jesus' twelve disciples and is often regarded as a traitor. According to the gospels of the New Testament, he betrayed Jesus to the Jewish authorities for 30 pieces of silver. This ultimately led to Jesus' arrest, crucifixion and death. The motives of Judas' betrayal are disputed, but it is assumed that he acted either for financial reasons or due to disappointment in Jesus' claim to be the Messiah.

The denial: The denial refers to the event in which Peter, one of Jesus' closest disciples, denied Jesus three times after he was arrested. Although Peter had previously declared that he was prepared to die with Jesus, he denied him out of fear of persecution and to protect his own life. After the third denial, Peter remembered Jesus' prediction and burst into tears.

Both Judas' betrayal and Peter's denial are tragic events in the context of Jesus' suffering and death. They show human weakness and failure, but also the importance of repentance and forgiveness. While Judas was unable to overcome his betrayal and eventually took his own life, Peter later received forgiveness from Jesus and became an important figure in the early church.

These events serve as a reminder that even Jesus' closest disciples made mistakes and that we as believers are also susceptible to temptation and weakness. They also remind us of the importance of repentance, forgiveness and the grace of God that enables us to recognize our mistakes, repent and live a new life in Christ.

CHAPTER 20

Before the cock crows three times.

After Jesus was arrested, he was brought before the high priestly court. During this time, Peter stood outside in the courtyard and was asked by various people about his connection to Jesus. Each time Peter denied that he knew Jesus or had any connection with him. Finally, he heard the rooster crowing and remembered Jesus' prediction that he would deny him three times before the rooster crowed.

Peter burst into tears and deeply regretted his actions. This episode shows the human weakness and failure of even a close disciple of Jesus. It also illustrates the importance of repentance and forgiveness. Later, after his resurrection, Jesus met Peter by the Sea of Galilee and gave him the opportunity to confess his love for him three times in order to make amends for his denial.

Peter's denial is an important part of the Passion story, reminding us that we as believers are also fallible and can sometimes fail. However, it also shows the mercy and grace of Jesus, who always gives us the opportunity to recognize our mistakes, repent and restore a relationship with him.

CHAPTER 21

How old was Jesus?

The symbolic meaning of Jesus being 33 years old at the time of his crucifixion is discussed in various theological and spiritual interpretations. Here are some possible meanings:

Perfection: In some traditions, the age of 33 is seen as a symbol of perfection or maturity. It is assumed that Jesus had fulfilled his mission at this time and was spiritually perfect.

Connection with the Old Testament: The age of 33 is sometimes associated with the number 3, which has a symbolic meaning in a biblical context. The number 3 stands for completeness, wholeness or divine perfection. Jesus was often regarded as the "new Adam" who corrected the mistakes of the first man. Adam is traditionally estimated to be around 30 years old, and the age of 33 could indicate that Jesus fulfilled this role completely.

Sacrifice and redemption: The age of 33 can also be associated with Jesus' sacrifice on the cross. Some interpretations argue that this was the ideal age for an atoning sacrifice and that Jesus deliberately reached this age in order to give his life as a sacrifice for the sins of mankind.

It is important to note that this symbolic meaning is not uniform in all Christian traditions and that there are different interpretations. Ultimately, the exact symbolic meaning of Jesus' age of 33 at the time of his crucifixion remains subject to theological discussion and individual interpretation.

CHAPTER 22

The crucifixion

Sacrifice: The crucifixion symbolizes the ultimate sacrifice of Jesus Christ for humanity. Jesus voluntarily gave his life on the cross to bear the sins of the world and make redemption possible. His sacrifice is seen as an expression of God's unconditional love.

Forgiveness: The crucifixion also symbolizes the forgiveness of sins through Jesus Christ. Through his death on the cross, he offers people the opportunity to repent of their sins and receive forgiveness from God. The cross reminds us that we are all sinners and that we can find forgiveness and reconciliation with God through faith in Jesus Christ.

Redemption: The cross also symbolizes redemption through Jesus Christ. Through his death and resurrection, he has power over death and enables believers to live a new life in communion with God. The cross reminds us that through faith in Jesus Christ we can be freed from the power of sin and have eternal life with God.

Love: The cross is a symbol of God's unconditional love for mankind. It shows that God was willing to sacrifice his son in order to save us and to enter into a relationship with him. The cross reminds us that we are loved and that we are called upon to show this love to others.

Hope: The cross also symbolizes hope for those who believe in Jesus Christ. It reminds us that despite the suffering and difficulties in this world, there is hope for eternal life with God. The cross encourages us to place our hope in Jesus Christ and trust that he will lead us through all of life's challenges.

The symbol of the crucifixion is a central element of the Christian faith and is used in churches, devotions and personal prayers. It reminds believers of the sacrifice, forgiveness, redemption, love and hope represented by Jesus Christ on the cross.

CHAPTER 23

The robe

Unity and perfection: Jesus' robe is described in the Gospels as seamless, which indicates that there was no separation or division. It symbolizes the unity and perfection of Jesus Christ as the Son of God. It shows his divine nature and his perfect purity.

Dignity and honor: The robe also represents the dignity and honor of Jesus. In biblical times, wearing a seamless robe was a sign of prestige and dignity. By dividing his garment among themselves, the soldiers literally stripped Jesus of his clothes and robbed him of his dignity. This illustrates the humiliation he suffered during his crucifixion.

Prophecy fulfillment: The dividing of the garment fulfilled an Old Testament prophecy from Psalm 22:19: "They have divided my garments among them, and cast lots for my clothing." This prophecy pointed to the suffering and betrayal of Jesus.

Solidarity with the suffering: Jesus' robe can also be seen as a symbol of his solidarity with those who suffer. Through his exposure, he shows his identification with the poor, the oppressed and the vulnerable. It reminds us that Jesus himself took upon himself the suffering and pain of humanity.

Sacrifice and redemption: The robe can also be associated with sacrifice and redemption through Jesus. By laying down his robe, Jesus gives up everything to bear the sins of the world and make redemption possible. It symbolizes his selfless act of love and devotion for humanity.

The robe of Jesus has a deep symbolic meaning in the Passion of Christ. It represents unity, perfection, dignity, fulfillment of prophecy, solidarity with the suffering, sacrifice and redemption. It reminds us of Jesus' suffering and sacrifice for us and calls us to follow him and reflect his love and mercy in the world.

CHAPTER 24

The crown of thorns

Suffering and sacrifice: The crown of thorns symbolizes the suffering and pain that Jesus endured during his Passion. It was put on him by the Roman soldiers to mock and humiliate him. The sharp thorns penetrated his scalp and caused great pain. The crown of thorns reminds us that Jesus was prepared to lay down his life as a sacrifice for the sins of the world.

Kingship: Although the crown of thorns was originally intended as a sign of mockery, it also has an ironic symbolic meaning of Jesus' kingship. During the crucifixion, Jesus was given a shield that read: "Jesus of Nazareth, King of the Jews". The crown of thorns can be seen as an ironic sign of this royal rule. It shows that Jesus reigns as king over the kingdom of God, even though his reign is not recognized or accepted by the people.

Sin and curse: The crown of thorns can also be linked to the biblical theme of sin and the curse. Genesis tells us that after the fall of man, Adam and Eve were confronted with thorns and thistles (Genesis 3:18). The crown of thorns reminds us that Jesus took the consequences of sin upon himself and broke the curse. Through his suffering and death on the cross, he offers redemption from sin and deliverance from its curse.

Humility and devotion: The crown of thorns also symbolizes Jesus' humility and devotion. Although he came as King of Heaven, he voluntarily took on the form of a servant and submitted to the suffering and shame of the cross. The crown of thorns reminds us that true power lies in humility and devotion.

Victory over death: Finally, the crown of thorns can also be seen as a symbol of victory over death. Although Jesus died on the cross, he was raised from the dead and conquered death. The crown of thorns points to suffering, but also to the hope of resurrection and eternal life with God.

The crown of thorns is a powerful symbol of Christ's passion. It represents the suffering and sacrifice of Jesus, his royal kingship despite being mocked, deliverance from sin and curse, humility and devotion, and victory over death. It reminds us of Jesus' sacrifice for our redemption and calls us to follow him and reflect his love and devotion in our own lives.

CHAPTER 25

The crucifixion as the resolution of the hereditary guilt of the Old Testament

Sacrifice and redemption: The crucifixion symbolizes Jesus' ultimate sacrifice for the redemption of mankind. Jesus voluntarily gave his life on the cross to bear the sins of the world and to open the way for people to be reconciled with God. His death on the cross is seen as the perfect sacrifice that wipes away humanity's guilt before God.

Love and forgiveness: The crucifixion is a powerful sign of God's unconditional love for humanity. Jesus died on the cross to redeem us from our sins, even though we did not deserve it. His love and forgiveness are clearly visible in his sacrifice on the cross. The message of the crucifixion calls us to accept this love and to pass it on in our own lives.

Suffering and solidarity: The crucifixion also shows the suffering of Jesus and his solidarity with those who suffer. Jesus was tortured, mocked and crucified, which gives a deep insight into human suffering. Through his own suffering, he shows his identification with the poor, the oppressed and the vulnerable. The message of the crucifixion calls us to show compassion and solidarity with those who suffer and to stand up for justice and mercy.

Victory over sin and death: The crucifixion also symbolizes Jesus' victory over sin and death. Although Jesus died on the cross, he was raised from the dead and conquered death. His sacrifice on the cross opens the way to eternal communion with God and gives us hope for life after death. The message of the crucifixion is a message of victory over evil and the hope of eternal life.

Humility and devotion: The crucifixion also shows the humility and devotion of Jesus. Although he came as the Son of God, he voluntarily took on the form of a servant and submitted himself to the suffering and shame of the cross. His humility and devotion are an example to us of how we can give our own lives in love and service to others.

The crucifixion of Jesus Christ has a profound symbolic meaning and message. It represents sacrifice and redemption, the unconditional love and forgiveness of God, the suffering and solidarity of Jesus, victory over sin and death, and humility and surrender. The message of the crucifixion calls us to live this love, forgiveness, solidarity, hope, humility and devotion in our own lives and to pass it on in the world.

The crucifixion of Jesus is often seen as a repetition of the original sin of the Old Testament. The Old Testament tells us that Adam and Eve sinned against God's commandment in the Garden of Eden, thereby passing on original sin to the whole of humanity. This original sin separated mankind from God and led to a broken relationship between God and mankind.

The crucifixion of Jesus is seen as the ultimate sacrifice made to atone for inherited guilt and restore the relationship between God and man. Jesus, who is regarded as the Son of God, voluntarily took upon himself the suffering and death of the cross to bear the sins of the world. Through his sacrifice on the cross, the sins of mankind were blotted out before God and an opportunity for reconciliation was created.

The crucifixion of Jesus is often referred to as the "Lamb of God" who was sacrificed to take away the sins of the world. This term comes from the Old Testament, where lambs were used as sacrificial animals to atone for sins. Jesus is seen as the perfect sacrifice that fulfills and surpasses all previous sacrifices in the Old Testament.

The crucifixion of Jesus is also associated with the Passover, a

Jewish festival that commemorates the exodus of the Israelites from Egypt. During Passover, a lamb was sacrificed to put blood on the doorposts and save the Israelites from the angel of death. Jesus is often seen as the "Passover lamb" whose blood frees us from the power of death.

Jesus' crucifixion as reparation for the inherited guilt of the Old Testament emphasizes the importance of his sacrifice for the redemption of humanity. Through his suffering and death on the cross, Jesus offers an opportunity for reconciliation with God and liberation from sin. It is an act of God's grace and love that gives us the hope of eternal life.

CHAPTER 26

The spear

The spear mentioned in connection with the cross of Jesus also has a symbolic meaning. According to the Gospels, a Roman soldier pierced Jesus' side with a spear after he died on the cross. This event is often seen as the fulfillment of a prophetic scripture that says: "They will look upon him whom they have pierced" (Zechariah 12:10).

The piercing with the spear symbolizes various aspects:

Confirmation of death: The piercing with the spear confirmed Jesus' death. In Roman practice, this was sometimes done to ensure that the crucified man was actually dead. This event thus testifies to the reality of Jesus' death and his complete sacrifice for the sins of the world.

Sacrifice and redemption: The piercing with the spear can also be seen as a symbol of Jesus' sacrifice and his act of redemption. The blood and water that flowed from his side is often seen as a symbol of the life and grace given through his sacrifice on the cross. It reminds us of the precious gift of redemption and the possibility of reconciliation with God.

Unity of the Church: Some theologians also see the piercing with the spear as a symbol of the unity of the Church. The blood and water that flowed from Jesus' side is sometimes seen as a symbol of the sacraments of baptism and the Eucharist. These sacraments are central elements of the Christian faith and serve to unite the faithful in communion with Christ and with each other.

Fulfillment of scripture: The piercing with the spear also fulfills a prophetic passage from the Old Testament (Zechariah 12:10).

This shows that Jesus' death on the cross was part of the divine plan and that he fulfilled the promises of the Holy Scriptures.

The spear that pierced Jesus' side therefore has a symbolic meaning in connection with his death on the cross. It confirms his death, symbolizes his sacrifice and his act of redemption, emphasizes the unity of the Church and fulfils prophetic scriptural passages. Overall, the spear reminds us that Jesus voluntarily gave his life for us and that his sacrifice gives us hope for redemption and eternal life.

CHAPTER 27

Burial and resurrection

The burial of Jesus and his resurrection are central events in the Christian faith. Here is a detailed explanation of the symbolic meaning of these events:

Burial of Jesus:
The burial of Jesus symbolizes the end of his earthly life and his death on the cross. After Jesus died on the cross, his body was taken down from the cross and placed in a tomb. The burial shows the reality of Jesus' death and reminds us that he was truly human and experienced the pain and suffering of the world.

The burial of Jesus also symbolizes the transience of human life and the finite nature of earthly existence. It reminds us that we are all mortal and that death is a part of human life.

Resurrection of Jesus:
The resurrection of Jesus symbolizes his triumphant overcoming of death and his power over life. According to the Gospels, Jesus was raised from the dead three days after his burial. His resurrection shows that death does not have the last word, but that there is hope for eternal life.

The resurrection of Jesus also symbolizes the promise of resurrection for all believers. In the Christian faith, the resurrection is seen as a sign of hope for eternal life with God. It reminds us that our faith in Jesus Christ unites us with him and that through his death and resurrection we have the opportunity to share in his eternal life.

The resurrection of Jesus also symbolizes the victory over sin and evil. Through his death on the cross, Jesus bore the sins of the world and through his resurrection he conquered death. The resurrection is a sign of liberation from the power of sin and death and an expression of divine grace and love.

Symbolic meaning:
The burial of Jesus and his resurrection have a profound symbolic meaning in the Christian faith:

They symbolize redemption and reconciliation with God. Through his death on the cross, Jesus atoned for the sins of the world and gave us the opportunity to be reconciled with God. His resurrection shows that this redemption is real and that we can have new life in communion with God through our faith in him.

They symbolize the hope of eternal life. The resurrection of Jesus gives us hope for life after death. It reminds us that death is not the end, but that there is a continuation of life with God.

They symbolize the victory over evil and the power of death. The resurrection of Jesus shows that evil and death do not have the last word, but that God's love and grace are stronger. It encourages us to fight against evil and to have hope in the midst of suffering and death.

There are different theological interpretations of the resurrection of Jesus, including the question of whether it is to be understood physically or spiritually. Some theologians emphasize the physical resurrection of Jesus, while others speak more of a spiritual resurrection. Here is a detailed explanation of the symbolic meaning of the spiritual resurrection:

Transformation and new life: The spiritual resurrection of Jesus symbolizes a profound transformation and a new life. It shows that Jesus not only overcame death, but also experienced a change in his existence. This change can be understood as a spiritual renewal or as an ascent to a higher level of being.

Symbol of rebirth: Spiritual resurrection can also be seen as a symbol of rebirth. It reminds us that we can receive a new life through our faith in Jesus Christ. Just as Jesus rose from the dead, we too can experience a new life in communion with God through faith in him.

Spiritual dimension: The spiritual resurrection emphasizes the spiritual dimension of the Christian faith. It shows that the kingdom of God does not only exist in this world, but is also a supernatural reality. The spiritual resurrection gives us a glimpse of eternal life and encourages us to place our hope in the afterlife.

Symbol for overcoming death: The spiritual resurrection of Jesus also symbolizes the overcoming of death and transience. It reminds us that death does not have the last word, but that there is hope for life after death. Through his resurrection, Jesus shows that life in God is infinite and that death is only a temporary separation from God.

Symbol for the connection with God: The spiritual resurrection emphasizes the close connection between Jesus and God. It shows that Jesus, as the Son of God, has a unique relationship with God and that we can also be in communion with God through our faith in him. The spiritual resurrection gives us the opportunity to experience a deep spiritual connection with God.

The spiritual resurrection of Jesus therefore has a symbolic meaning that encompasses transformation and new life, rebirth, a spiritual dimension, overcoming death and connection with God. It reminds us that our faith in Jesus Christ can lead us to profound change and that through him we have hope for eternal life.

CHAPTER 28

Why are there different gospels?

There are different gospels in the New Testament because they were written by different authors at different times and for different communities. Each gospel has its own perspective, focus and target audience. Here are some reasons why there are different gospels:

Different target groups: The Gospels were written for different communities and target groups. For example, the Gospel of Matthew was mainly addressed to a Jewish-Christian community, while the Gospel of Luke was addressed to a Greek-speaking audience. The authors adapted their texts accordingly to meet the needs and background of their respective target groups.

Different emphases: Each gospel places a different emphasis on certain aspects of Jesus' life and teachings. For example, the Gospel of John emphasizes the divine nature of Jesus and his relationship with the Father, while the Gospel of Luke focuses on the mercy of Jesus and his care for the poor and outcasts. These different emphases reflect the theological convictions and interests of the respective authors.

Oral tradition: The Gospels are based on the oral tradition of the stories about Jesus. In the first decades after Jesus' death, his words and deeds were passed on orally before they were recorded in writing. During this time, variations in the stories could develop, depending on who was telling them and for what purpose. The evangelists then recorded this oral tradition in written form, adding their own perspectives and interpretations.

Theological perspectives: The evangelists had different

theological perspectives and intentions when writing their texts. They not only wanted to tell the story of Jesus, but also to convey certain theological messages. For example, the Gospel of Mark emphasizes the importance of Jesus' suffering and discipleship, while the Gospel of Matthew emphasizes Jesus' fulfillment of Old Testament prophecies. These different theological perspectives reflect the diversity of the early Christian communities.

It is important to note that these differences in the Gospels do not mean that they contradict each other or that one version is "more correct" than the other. Rather, they offer different perspectives on the life and teachings of Jesus and complement each other to provide a more comprehensive understanding. The diversity of the Gospels in the New Testament demonstrates the breadth and depth of the Christian faith and allows believers to explore different aspects of Jesus' life and message.

CHAPTER 29

Gospel of Thomas

The Gospel of Thomas is one of the apocryphal writings that are not included in the canonical Gospels of the New Testament. It is a collection of 114 sayings or logia that are attributed to Jesus. The Gospel of Thomas was first discovered in the 20th century and probably dates back to the 2nd century.

The sayings in the Gospel of Thomas are often formulated in the form of short pieces of wisdom or riddles. They deal with various topics such as spirituality, knowledge, the Kingdom of God and the search for truth. In contrast to the canonical gospels, the Gospel of Thomas does not contain any narrative stories about the life of Jesus or his deeds.

Some of the most famous sayings in the Gospel of Thomas are:

"If you do not fast your eyes, you will not see the kingdom of God."

"He who seeks will not stop seeking until he finds; and when he finds, he will be shaken; and when he is shaken, he will be astonished and will rule over the universe."

"Jesus said: I am the light that is above all. I am everything: from me all things came forth, and to me all things returned. Split a piece of wood: I am there; pick up a stone: You will find me there."

It is important to note that the Gospel of Thomas is considered a Gnostic work by many theologians and biblical scholars. Gnosticism was a religious movement in early Christianity that was characterized by its emphasis on spiritual insight and knowledge. The Gospel of Thomas therefore contains some Gnostic elements and teachings.

It is also worth noting that the Gospel of Thomas is not recognized as an authoritative source by most Christian traditions. It is often regarded as an interesting historical or theological supplement, but not as part of the canonical New Testament.

CHAPTER 30

Newly discovered gospels

There are some mentions of erased or lost parts of the New Testament that appear in some historical sources. These texts are often referred to as apocryphal or pseudo-bigraphical writings and are not part of the canonical New Testament.

One example of an erased text is the Gospel according to Jude, which is said to have been written in the 2nd century. It was only rediscovered in 2006 when a Coptic version of the text emerged. The Gospel according to Judas allegedly contains dialogues between Jesus and Judas Iscariot, in which Judas is portrayed as the one who facilitated Jesus' betrayal in order to fulfil his divine mission.

Another example is the Gospel according to Mary Magdalene, which is mentioned in some Gnostic writings. It is claimed that this gospel was written by Mary Magdalene herself and emphasizes her special relationship with Jesus. It allegedly contains teachings and revelations that Jesus is said to have entrusted only to Mary Magdalene.

There are also other apocryphal writings such as the Gospel of Thomas, the Infancy Gospel of Thomas or the Gospel of Peter, which contain additional stories about Jesus and his disciples. However, these writings were not included in the canonical text and are not considered authoritative sources by most Christian traditions.It is important to note that the decision to include or reject certain texts in the canonical New Testaments depends on various factors, such as theological consistency, historical reliability and connection to the apostolic tradition. The choice of canonical text has been made by ecclesiastical authorities over the centuries and is subject to further discussion and debate among theologians and biblical scholars.

CHAPTER 31

The Revelation of John

The Revelation of John is the last book of the New Testament and contains a series of visions and prophecies revealed to the apostle John. It is a highly symbolic and apocalyptic book that deals with end-time themes, the battle between good and evil, and the ultimate rule of God over the world. Here are some important aspects of the Revelation of John:

Author: The book is traditionally attributed to the apostle John, who also wrote the Gospel of John. However, there is some debate among scholars about the exact identity of the author.

Apocalyptic literature: The Revelation of John belongs to apocalyptic literature, which was widespread in the Jewish tradition. Apocalyptic texts are characterized by their symbolic language, their depiction of heavenly visions and their prophetic messages.

Visions and symbols: The book consists of a series of visions that John receives while he is imprisoned on the island of Patmos. These visions are full of symbolic images such as seven seals, seven trumpets, four horsemen of the apocalypse and the beast from the sea. These symbols represent different aspects of end-time events and spiritual realities.

End-time themes: The Revelation of John deals with a variety of end-time themes such as the battle between good and evil, the judgment of God on the world, the restoration of creation and the introduction of the kingdom of God. It also describes the persecution of believers, the Antichrist and the last judgment.

Message of hope: Although the Revelation of John contains

many dark and frightening images, its basic message is one of hope. It emphasizes that God will ultimately prevail and that evil will be defeated. It encourages believers to remain steadfast in faith and hope in the coming reign of God.

Theological interpretations: The Revelation of John has been subject to various theological interpretations throughout history. Some see it as a literal prophecy of future events, while others see it as a symbolic representation of timeless spiritual truths. There are also differing views on the exact sequence of events in the end times.

The Revelation of John is a challenging book that raises many questions and allows for different interpretations. It challenges readers to reflect on the meaning of suffering, faith and hope and reminds us that God is ultimately above all and will realize his plans for the world.

CHAPTER 32

The symbolic meaning of the Revelation of John

Numbers: Various numbers are used in Revelation that have symbolic meanings. For example, the number seven stands for completeness and perfection, as it is often mentioned in connection with the seven churches, the seven seals and the seven trumpets. The number twelve stands for the twelve tribes of Israel or the twelve apostles and symbolizes the completeness of God's people.

Animals: Various animals are mentioned in Revelation that have symbolic meanings. The lamb represents Jesus Christ as the sacrificial lamb who was sacrificed for the sins of the world. The dragon represents Satan or evil, while the beast from the sea represents the Antichrist. These animals symbolize the battle between good and evil.

Colors: Revelation also uses different colors that have symbolic meanings. White stands for purity and holiness, while red stands for bloodshed and persecution. Black symbolizes mourning and darkness, while gold stands for divine glory and riches.

Heaven and earth: Revelation also uses images of heaven and earth to represent spiritual realities. Heaven represents the presence of God and the kingdom of God, while earth symbolizes the world and earthly life. Revelation shows that there is a connection between heaven and earth and that God's reign will ultimately be established on earth.

Judgment and redemption: Revelation also contains images of judgment and redemption. Judgment is often represented by images of fire, destruction and punishment, while redemption is represented by images of salvation, healing and restoration. These images show the battle between good and evil and emphasize the hope for a just world order.

It is important to note that these symbols in Revelation should not be taken literally, but as metaphorical representations of spiritual truths. They serve to illustrate complex theological concepts and help readers grasp deeper spiritual meaning. The symbolic language of Revelation challenges readers to reflect on their own ideas about God, evil and the end times and opens up new perspectives on faith.

CHAPTER 33

The Lamb of God

Old Testament: In the Old Testament, the sacrificial lamb is used as a symbol of atonement and forgiveness. In the Book of Exodus, God instructs the Israelites to slaughter a one-year-old, unblemished lamb and to paint its blood on the doorposts of their houses to protect them from the angel of death. This event is celebrated as Passover and commemorates the liberation of the Israelites from slavery in Egypt. The sacrificial lamb thus symbolizes salvation, redemption and protection.

John the Baptist: In the New Testament, the Lamb of God is first mentioned by John the Baptist. When Jesus comes to him, John says: "Behold, the Lamb of God who takes away the sin of the world!" (John 1:29). With this statement, John is referring to Jesus, who came as the ultimate sacrificial lamb to bear the sins of mankind and bring them redemption.

Jesus as the sacrificial lamb: The use of the symbol of the Lamb of God for Jesus emphasizes his role as the perfect sacrifice for the sins of mankind. Like the Passover lamb in the Old Testament, Jesus was offered as a spotless and innocent sacrifice to bear the punishment for our sins. His death on the cross is seen as the ultimate sacrificial lamb that takes away the sin of the world and opens the way to forgiveness and reconciliation with God.

Symbol of humility and gentleness: The lamb is also a symbol of humility and gentleness. Jesus is often referred to as the "Lamb of God" to emphasize his humble and gentle nature. He taught people to be humble, to serve one another and to refrain from violence. The lamb therefore also symbolizes the virtues of gentleness, peace and love.

Victory over evil: Finally, the Lamb of God symbolizes victory over evil and death. In the Revelation of John, Jesus is depicted as the Lamb who stands in the midst of the heavenly throne and has dominion over the world. Through his death and resurrection, Jesus has achieved victory over the powers of darkness and offers believers the hope of eternal life.

The symbol of the Lamb of God is therefore rich in meaning and refers to various aspects of the Christian faith such as redemption, forgiveness, humility, meekness and victory over evil. It reminds us that Jesus Christ is the perfect sacrificial lamb who frees us from our sins and enables us to have a new relationship with God.

CHAPTER 34

Behold the Lamb of God bearing the sin of the world

The phrase "Behold the Lamb of God who takes away the sin of the world" comes from the New Testament, more precisely from the Gospel of John (John 1:29). Here, John the Baptist is quoted as seeing Jesus and saying: "Behold, the Lamb of God who takes away the sin of the world!"

This statement has a deeply symbolic meaning and contains several important aspects:

The Lamb of God: The lamb is a symbol of purity, innocence and sacrifice. It represents Jesus Christ as the chosen sacrificial lamb of God, who was prepared to lay down his life to bear the sins of the world.

The sin of the world: The expression "the sin of the world" refers to the collective guilt and depravity of humanity. It indicates that all people are sinners and are separated from God. The Lamb of God is presented as the means by which this sin can be overcome and forgiven.

Bearing sin: The statement emphasizes that Jesus was willing to take the burden of sin upon himself and bear it. Through his death on the cross, he takes the punishment for our sins upon himself and thus gives us access to forgiveness and reconciliation with God.

Taking away sin: The Lamb of God is presented as the means by which the sin of the world is taken away. This means not only that sins are forgiven, but also that the power and effects of sin are broken. Jesus enables us to live a new life in communion with God.

This statement by John the Baptist therefore emphasizes the

central role of Jesus Christ as the chosen sacrificial lamb of God, who was prepared to bear and overcome the sin of the world. It opens up the possibility of forgiveness, reconciliation and a new life in communion with God. It is a reminder of God's unconditional love and his willingness to redeem us.

CHAPTER 35

The Seven Seals

The exact meaning of the Seven Seals is subject to different interpretations and interpretations. However, here are some general aspects associated with the seals:

Mysterious Revelation: The Seven Seals symbolize a mysterious revelation or unveiling of events that will take place in the future. Each seal is opened in turn, revealing a new phase or event in the end times.

Judgments and disasters: The opening of the first four seals brings various judgments and disasters upon the earth. This includes wars, famines, plagues and death. These events are seen as signs of the coming judgment.

Martyrs and persecution: The fifth seal reveals the image of martyrs who died for their faith in Jesus Christ. It symbolizes persecution and suffering for believers during the end times.

Natural disasters: The sixth seal brings natural disasters such as earthquakes, cosmic phenomena and darkness upon the earth. These events are seen as signs of the imminent end.

Temporary rest: After the opening of the first six seals, there is a temporary rest before the seventh seal is opened. This seal contains further prophecies and events that are described in the following chapters of Revelation.

The exact interpretation of the Seven Seals can vary according to theological interpretation. Some see them as a symbolic representation of historical events, while others see them as a prophetic preview of future events. In either case, however, the Seven Seals represent an important message about the end times and the coming reign of God.

CHAPTER 36

The Trinity

The symbolic meaning of Jesus' age of 33 at the time of his crucifixion is discussed in various theological and spiritual interpretations. Here are some possible meanings:

Perfection: In some traditions, the age of 33 is seen as a symbol of perfection or maturity. It is assumed that Jesus had fulfilled his mission at this time and was spiritually perfect.

Connection with the Old Testament: The age of 33 is sometimes associated with the number 3, which has a symbolic meaning in a biblical context. The number 3 stands for completeness, wholeness or divine perfection. Jesus was often regarded as the "new Adam" who corrected the mistakes of the first man. Adam is traditionally estimated to be around 30 years old, and the age of 33 could indicate that Jesus fulfilled this role completely.

Sacrifice and redemption: The age of 33 can also be associated with Jesus' sacrifice on the cross. Some interpretations argue that this was the ideal age for an atoning sacrifice and that Jesus deliberately reached this age in order to give his life as a sacrifice for the sins of mankind.

It is important to note that this symbolic meaning is not uniform in all Christian traditions and that there are different interpretations. Ultimately, the exact symbolic meaning of Jesus' age of 33 at the time of his crucifixion remains subject to theological discussion and individual interpretation.

CHAPTER 37

The Holy Grail

The Holy Grail is a symbol of great significance and mysticism that plays a role in the Arthurian legend and in the Christian faith. There are various interpretations and theories about the symbolic meaning of the Holy Grail. Divine grace and redemption: The Holy Grail is often seen as a symbol of divine grace and redemption. In Christian tradition, the Grail is associated with the chalice that Jesus used at the Last Supper. It symbolizes the blood of Christ that was shed for the sins of mankind. The Grail reminds us that we can find redemption and forgiveness through faith in Jesus Christ.

Spiritual quest and transformation: The Holy Grail is also seen as a symbol of the spiritual quest for truth, wisdom and enlightenment. In the Arthurian legends, the Knights of the Round Table set out in search of the Grail, which represents their individual spiritual journey. The Grail symbolizes inner transformation and the pursuit of a deep connection with the divine.

Perfection and wholeness: The Holy Grail can also be seen as a symbol of perfection and wholeness. In some versions of the legend, it is said that the Grail is not only a chalice, but also a bowl or stone with healing powers. This symbolism indicates that the Grail is a source of spiritual nourishment and fulfillment that leads us to a complete and fulfilled existence.

Feminine energy and sacredness: In some interpretations, the Holy Grail is associated with feminine energy and sacredness. The Grail is sometimes considered to symbolize the sacred womb or womb of the Goddess. This symbolism emphasizes the importance of the feminine in spirituality and reminds us that both masculine and feminine energies should be united in our quest for the divine.

Mystery and unattainability: The Holy Grail is often portrayed as something mysterious and unattainable. In the Arthurian legends, the Grail often remains hidden or unattainable to those who are not worthy. This symbolism reminds us that the divine is often beyond our understanding and that we need humility and surrender to experience it.

The symbolic meaning of the Holy Grail can vary depending on the cultural context and individual interpretation. Overall, however, it often represents divine grace and redemption, spiritual quest and transformation, perfection and wholeness, feminine energy and sacredness, and mystery and unattainability. The Holy Grail encourages us to embark on our own spiritual journey, to search for truth and to find a deeper connection with the divine.

CHAPTER 38

Confrontation, Jesus as Savior

Sacrificial lamb: Jesus is often seen as the sacrificial lamb that was sacrificed for the sins of mankind. This symbolism goes back to the Old Testament, in which lambs were offered as sacrifices to obtain forgiveness and reconciliation with God. Jesus is seen as the ultimate sacrificial lamb, whose death on the cross wipes away the sins of the world and opens the way to redemption.

Holy chalice: In Christian tradition, Jesus is often associated with a holy chalice that was used at the Last Supper. This chalice symbolizes his shed blood, which stands for the forgiveness of sins. The chalice also represents the Eucharist or Lord's Supper, where believers consume bread and wine to remember Jesus' sacrifice and experience his presence in their lives.

Crucifixion and resurrection: The crucifixion and resurrection of Jesus are central events in the Christian faith and are often seen as symbols of redemption. The cross symbolizes the suffering and death of Jesus, while the resurrection represents his conquest of death and victory over sin. This symbolism emphasizes the hope of eternal life and the possibility of forgiveness and reconciliation through faith in Jesus Christ.

Shepherd and sheep: Jesus is also often seen as the good shepherd who leads and protects his sheep. This symbolism goes back to the image of the shepherd in the Old Testament, who lovingly cares for his flock. Jesus is seen as the one who protects us from danger, guides us and leads us into the paths of truth. This symbolism emphasizes Jesus' care and love for his followers.

Light of the world: Jesus is also seen as the light of the world that illuminates the darkness and shows the way to salvation. This symbolism emphasizes the spiritual enlightenment that can be achieved through faith in Jesus Christ. Jesus is seen as the light that dispels our darkness and leads us to a life of truth, love and hope.

The symbolic meaning of Jesus as Redeemer can vary depending on individual belief and theological interpretation. Overall, however, it often represents the sacrificial lamb, the holy chalice, the crucifixion and resurrection, the shepherd and the sheep, and the light of the world. Contemplating Jesus as Savior through these symbols encourages us to deepen our faith, seek forgiveness and strive to live in accordance with Jesus' teachings.

CHAPTER 39

The archangel

In the New Testament of the Christian faith, the archangel plays an important symbolic role. Here are some possible explanations for the symbolic meaning of the archangel:

Messenger of God: The archangel is often regarded as a messenger of God who delivers divine messages and serves as an intermediary between God and people. The word "archangel" literally means "chief angel" and indicates a high position and authority. The archangel symbolizes the connection between the divine and the human world.

Protection and guidance: The archangel is also seen as a symbol of protection and guidance. Various archangels are mentioned in the Bible, such as Michael, Gabriel and Raphael, each of whom has a specific role in protecting and guiding the faithful. The archangel symbolizes divine care and guidance in difficult times.

Fight against evil: In some biblical texts, the archangel is depicted as a warrior against evil. Michael in particular is often seen as the leader of the heavenly hosts who fights against Satan and his demons. The archangel symbolizes the victory of good over evil and encourages believers to oppose evil.

Annunciation: Another important symbol of the archangel is the proclamation of important events or messages. The archangel Gabriel is described in the New Testament as the angel who announces the birth of Jesus to Mary. This symbolism emphasizes the role of the archangel as the bearer of divine plans and revelations.

Healing and consolation: The archangel Raphael is often

associated with healing and consolation. In the biblical story of the Book of Tobit, Raphael accompanies the young Tobias on a journey and heals his father of blindness. The archangel symbolizes divine healing and the comfort that God gives to people.

The symbolic meaning of the archangel can vary depending on theological interpretation and individual belief. Overall, however, it often represents the messenger of God, protection and guidance, the fight against evil, the proclamation of important events as well as healing and comfort. Viewing the archangel through these symbols encourages us to entrust ourselves to divine guidance, to seek the good and to entrust ourselves to God's protection and care.

CHAPTER 40

Are Satan and the devil the same person?

In the New Testament of the Christian faith, both Satan and the devil are used as terms to describe evil and the adversary of God. Although the two terms are often used interchangeably, there are some differences in their meaning and usage. Here are some possible differences between Satan and devil in the New Testament:

Origin: In the New Testament, Satan is often referred to as the name of the fallen angel who rebelled against God and was banished from heaven. The devil, on the other hand, is seen more as a name for his role as a tempter and accuser.

Function: Satan is often portrayed in the New Testament as the accuser or tempter who tempts people to sin against God. He is also referred to as the "prince of this world", who has power over earthly reality. The devil, on the other hand, is more associated with the concept of evil and destruction.

Characterization: Satan is often portrayed as an intelligent and cunning opponent of God who tries to dissuade believers from their faith. The devil, on the other hand, is seen more as a personified force of evil that tempts people to sin.

Designations: Various names are used for Satan and the devil in the New Testament. Satan is also referred to as "the adversary", "the dragon" or "the old serpent". The devil is often referred to as "the tempter" or "the father of lies".

Eschatological significance: In the New Testament, both Satan and the devil are associated with the end-time scenario. They are seen as those who will be defeated at the end of time and thrown into eternal fire forever.

It is important to note that the distinction between Satan and the devil is not always clear in the New Testament and that the terms are sometimes used interchangeably. The exact meaning and usage depends on theological interpretation and interpretation. Overall, both Satan and the devil represent evil and the adversary of God in the New Testament.

CHAPTER 41

Satan and the devil outside the New Testament

Outside of the Christian faith, the terms Satan and devil can have different meanings, as they appear in different religious and philosophical traditions. Here are some possible considerations of Satan and the devil outside the Christian faith:

Judaism: In Judaism, Satan is often seen as an angel who is commissioned by God to test and accuse people. He is not seen as an evil or rebellious figure, but as a servant of God who fulfills his tasks. The term "devil" is used less in Judaism and refers more to the concept of evil in general.

Islam: In Islam, Satan is referred to as Iblis and is regarded as a fallen angel who rebelled against God's command. He is seen as a seducer who tempts people to sin against God. In Islam, the devil is often seen as a personified force of evil that tries to dissuade believers from the right path.

Buddhism: In Buddhism, there is no concept of a personal figure such as Satan or the devil. Instead, evil is seen as the result of ignorance and attachment. Buddhists emphasize the need to overcome one's ego and develop compassion in order to overcome suffering.

Hinduism: In Hinduism, there are various concepts of demons and evil spirits, which are regarded as embodiments of evil. These beings can take different forms and try to deceive or harm people. However, there is no specific figure such as Satan or the devil in the Christian sense.

It is important to note that these considerations of Satan and the devil outside the Christian faith are not exhaustive and that there may be different ideas in different religious traditions. The exact meaning and interpretation depends on the specific religious or philosophical tradition.

In some esoteric and gnostic traditions, Satan or the devil is seen as a symbol of the demiurge. The demiurge is a figure who, in some philosophical and religious systems, is seen as the creator god or world builder who created the material world. This idea is based on the assumption that the material world is considered inferior or illusory and that the Demiurge is not identical with the highest divine principle.

In this view, Satan or the Devil is often seen as a rebellious figure who rebels against the Demiurge and tries to free people from the illusion of the material world. Satan is then seen as a symbol of knowledge, freedom and liberation, while the Demiurge is seen as limitation and deception.

It is important to note that these ideas of Satan and the devil as a symbol of the demiurge are not found in traditional Christian belief. They are part of specific esoteric or gnostic teachings and represent alternative interpretations of religious symbols. The exact meaning and interpretation may vary depending on the esoteric tradition.

CHAPTER 42

Pontius Pilate

Pontius Pilate was a Roman prefect (procurator) of the province of Judea from 26 to 36 A.D. He is best known for his role in the condemnation and crucifixion of Jesus Christ.

The role of Pontius Pilate in the biblical narrative is closely linked to the trial and execution of Jesus. According to the gospels of the New Testament, Jesus was accused of blasphemy by the Jewish religious leaders, in particular the chief priests, and brought before Pilate for judgment.

As Roman governor, Pilate had the authority to decide over life and death. Although he initially found no guilt in Jesus, he eventually gave in to pressure from the Jewish crowd and condemned Jesus to death by crucifixion. He symbolically washed his hands to proclaim his innocence and shift the responsibility for the verdict onto the people.

The symbolism behind Pontius Pilate lies in his ambivalent role as political leader and judge. On the one hand, he shows a certain sympathy for Jesus and tries to release him; on the other, he ultimately gives in to the pressure of the crowd and condemns him to death. This reflects the tension between political calculation and moral responsibility.

Pilate's symbolic hand-washing has various interpretations. It can be seen as an attempt to wash himself clean of any guilt and to shift responsibility for the judgment onto others. It can also be interpreted as a sign of moral ambivalence and opportunism, as Pilate tries to maintain his own position and at the same time appease the crowd's displeasure.

In the Christian tradition, Pontius Pilate is often seen as a symbol of human weakness and the temptation to sacrifice moral principles in favor of political or personal interests. His role in the crucifixion of Jesus is seen as part of the divine plan for the redemption of humanity, in which Jesus voluntarily sacrifices his life to bear the sins of the world.

It is important to note that the historical accuracy of the portrayal of Pontius Pilate in the Gospels is disputed. There are limited extra-biblical sources about his time in office and his personality. Nevertheless, his role in the biblical narrative remains central to understanding the suffering and death of Jesus Christ in the Christian faith.

CHAPTER 43

Herod

King Herod, also known as Herod the Great, was an important political leader at the time of Jesus Christ. His symbolic significance lies in his role as ruler and his actions during his reign.

Herod was a king of the Jews who was appointed by the Romans. Although he himself was of Jewish descent, he had close ties to the Roman Empire and sought to consolidate his power and prestige by building great structures such as the Temple in Jerusalem.

Symbolically, Herod stands for ambitions for worldly power and wealth. He was known for his tyrannical rule and his willingness to eliminate anyone who posed a threat to his position - including members of his own family. This violence and paranoia reflect the dark side of human ambition.

In the biblical narrative, Herod plays a central role in connection with the birth of Jesus. When the wise men from the East asked for the newborn King of the Jews, Herod felt threatened and ordered the killing of all male children under the age of two in Bethlehem (the so-called "Massacre of the Innocents"). This event symbolizes the rejection of the divine plan for salvation by a power-hungry ruler.

Furthermore, Herod is often seen as a symbol of the rejection of the Messiah. Although he knew of the prophecies about the coming Messiah, he tried to kill Jesus in order to secure his own power. This contrasts with the humility and devotion of Jesus, who was prepared to sacrifice his life for the redemption of mankind.

The symbolic significance of Herod also lies in his role as the representative of a world power (Rome) and his oppression of the Jewish people. His reign is often seen as an example of corruption and oppression by worldly powers.

Overall, King Herod symbolizes the dark side of human ambitions for power, wealth and control. His actions contrast with the message of love, peace and redemption embodied by Jesus Christ. Through his rejection of the Messiah and his violent rule, Herod serves as a warning of the dangers of selfishness and greed for worldly power.

CHAPTER 44

Salome

Salome is a biblical figure mentioned in the Gospels of the New Testament. Her symbolic significance lies in her role as the embodiment of seduction, power and moral depravity.

Salome was the daughter of Herod Antipas and Herodias. In the biblical narrative, she is associated with the dance before Herod, where she impressed him so much that he granted her a wish. At her mother's instigation, Salome asked for the head of John the Baptist, who had previously rebuked Herod for his inappropriate relationship with Herodias.

Symbolically, Salome stands for the power of seduction and manipulation. Her dance before Herod is often depicted as a sensual and seductive event that awakens his desires and makes him fulfill an immoral wish. She uses her beauty and charm to achieve her goals.

Furthermore, Salome also symbolizes the exercise of power in an unethical way. By persuading Herod to behead the head of John the Baptist, she demonstrates her ability to influence political decisions and affect people's lives. This illustrates the danger of abuse of power and moral corruption.

Salome is also often associated with the idea of the femme fatale - a woman who leads men to their downfall through her beauty and seductive power. She is often seen as a symbol of seduction and the destruction of male virtue.

In art and literature, Salome is often portrayed as a figure who embodies sexual permissiveness and moral depravity. Her dance before Herod is often depicted as a sensual and provocative event that reveals the dark side of human nature.

The symbolic significance of Salome lies in her depiction of seduction, abuse of power and moral corruption. She serves as a warning against the dangers of temptation and the lure of the flesh. Her story is a reminder that the exercise of power without moral boundaries can lead to destructive consequences.

CHAPTER 45

Christian holidays

Christianity has a variety of holidays that celebrate important events in the life and ministry of Jesus Christ, as well as other significant aspects of the faith. Here are some of the most important Christian holidays and their meanings:

Christmas (December 25): Christmas celebrates the birth of Jesus Christ. It is a festival of joy and peace in which believers celebrate the incarnation of God in Jesus Christ.

Epiphany (January 6): The Epiphany marks the revelation of Jesus as the Son of God and the appearance of the star of Bethlehem, which led the wise men from the East to Jesus. It is often associated with the baptism of Jesus and Jesus' first miracle at the wedding in Cana.

Good Friday: Good Friday commemorates the death of Jesus on the cross for the forgiveness of humanity's sins. It is a day of mourning and reflection on which believers think about the suffering and sacrificial death of Jesus.

Easter: Easter is the most important festival in the Christian calendar and celebrates the resurrection of Jesus Christ from the dead. It symbolizes the victory over death and the redemption of mankind through Jesus' sacrifice on the cross.

Ascension: Ascension marks the return of Jesus to heaven, 40 days after his resurrection. It emphasizes the divine nature of Jesus and his rule over the universe.

Pentecost: Pentecost commemorates the outpouring of the Holy Spirit on the disciples of Jesus, 50 days after Easter. It symbolizes the strengthening and empowerment of believers through the

Holy Spirit.

All Saints' Day (November 1): All Saints' Day honors all the saints and martyrs of Christianity, known or unknown. It is a day to honor their virtues and remember their example.

Advent: Advent is a time of preparation and expectation for the coming of Jesus Christ. It begins four Sundays before Christmas and emphasizes the hope, love, joy and peace that Jesus brings to the world.

This list is not exhaustive, as there are many other regional and cultural variations of Christian holidays. Each of these celebrations has its own significance and serves to strengthen faith, promote fellowship and honor the life and work of Jesus Christ.

CHAPTER 46

The shroud of Jesus

The Shroud of Jesus, also known as the Shroud of Turin, is a piece of cloth that is said to have covered the face and body of Jesus after his crucifixion. There are many theories and controversies surrounding the authenticity and symbolic meaning of the Shroud. Here are some possible interpretations:

Passion and sacrifice: Jesus' shroud is often seen as a symbol of his passion and sacrifice. It reminds us of Jesus' painful crucifixion and death on the cross for the forgiveness of humanity's sins. The blood and stigmata on the shroud symbolize his suffering and sacrifice.

Resurrection and hope: Some believers see Jesus' shroud as a symbol of his resurrection from the dead. They believe that the shroud contains the traces of the resurrection, as it shows no remains or signs of decay. This symbolism emphasizes the hope of eternal life after death and the conquest of death through Jesus Christ.

Relic and veneration: The shroud of Jesus is regarded by many as a holy relic that is venerated with great reverence. It is seen as physical proof of the existence and work of Jesus. Veneration of the shroud can serve to strengthen faith and establish a deeper connection with Jesus.

Faith and doubt: Jesus' shroud also has a symbolic meaning with regard to faith and doubt. The controversy surrounding the authenticity of the shroud has led to differing opinions, which can lead to questions and doubts. It reminds us that faith is sometimes associated with uncertainty and challenges, but also offers the opportunity to have profound spiritual experiences.

Invitation to reflection: Regardless of its authenticity, Jesus' shroud serves as an invitation to reflect on life, death and the meaning of faith. It invites us to reflect on our own mortality and to consider the message of love, forgiveness and redemption that Jesus embodies.

The symbolic meaning of Jesus' shroud can vary depending on personal belief and interpretation. Overall, however, it often represents passion and sacrifice, resurrection and hope, relic and veneration, faith and doubt, and an invitation to reflection. The Shroud of Jesus reminds us that faith is not only dependent on rational evidence or physical relics, but also involves a personal relationship with Jesus Christ.

The following considerations are intended to discuss the roles of Jesus Christ in comparison to other religions or faiths.

CHAPTER 47

Jesus vs. Osiris

Parallels:

Birth and death: Both Jesus and Osiris have special birth stories. In the Christian faith, Jesus is born of a virgin, Mary, while in Egyptian mythology, Osiris is considered the son of the sky god Geb and the earth goddess Nut. Both figures also suffer a violent death - Jesus is crucified, while Osiris is murdered by his brother Seth.

Resurrection: A remarkable parallel between Jesus and Osiris is their resurrection. In Christianity, Jesus is raised from the dead three days after his death to promise eternal life. In Egyptian mythology, Osiris is also resurrected from the dead to rule over the afterlife.

Role as redeemer: Both Jesus and Osiris are seen as redeemer figures. In Christianity, Jesus is seen as the one who redeemed the sins of mankind through his death and resurrection and gives believers eternal life. In Egyptian mythology, Osiris is regarded as the ruler of the realm of the dead and offers people the possibility of redemption after death.

Differences:

Religious contexts: Jesus is a central figure in Christianity, a monotheistic religion that emphasizes the worship of a single God. Christianity is based on the teachings and beliefs written down in the Bible. Osiris, on the other hand, is a figure from Egyptian mythology, a polytheistic religion that worships a multitude of gods and goddesses.

Belief systems: Christianity emphasizes belief in an all-powerful God who created the world and rules over it. It emphasizes moral principles such as charity, forgiveness and mercy. Egyptian mythology was polytheistic and included a variety of gods and goddesses representing different aspects of life and nature.

Historicity: There are historical records about Jesus that prove his existence as a historical figure. The Gospels in the New Testament of the Bible contain accounts of his life, teachings, death and resurrection. Osiris, on the other hand, is considered a mythological figure for whom there is no direct historical evidence.

It is important to note that parallels can be found between Jesus and Osiris in some aspects of their stories, but their religious contexts, belief systems and historical significance differ significantly. While Jesus is a central figure in Christianity and is worshipped by millions of people as the son of God, Osiris is seen in Egyptian mythology as a deity who plays an important role in the cult of the dead and in the concept of the afterlife.

CHAPTER 48

Jesus and Buddha

The idea that Jesus was a Buddha is an interpretation that has been proposed by some people, but it is not supported by most Christian traditions. Both Jesus and the historical Buddha Siddhartha Gautama were religious leaders who lived in the 1st century BC and 5th century BC respectively and spread teachings about spirituality and enlightenment.

There are some parallels between the teachings of Jesus and Buddhism, such as the emphasis on charity, compassion and forgiveness. Both also emphasized the importance of inner peace and spiritual transformation.

Despite these similarities, however, there are also fundamental differences between Christianity and Buddhism. Christianity is based on the belief in Jesus Christ as the Son of God and Savior of humanity, while Buddhism does not worship a deity and focuses on individual liberation from suffering.

It is important to note that religious interpretations are often subjective and can depend on personal beliefs and experiences. The idea that Jesus was a Buddha or that there are similarities between their teachings may be meaningful to some people, but is not accepted or supported by all.

CHAPTER 49

Jesus and Islam.

Islam regards Jesus as one of the most important prophets and reveres him as a messenger of God. In the Quran, Jesus is referred to as Isa ibn Maryam (Jesus, son of Mary) and his birth, life and teachings are described in detail.

In Islam, Jesus is seen as a righteous prophet who was sent by God to proclaim the message of monotheism. Muslims believe that Jesus performed miracles, such as healing the sick and raising the dead. They also believe in his virgin birth through Mary.

However, there are some differences between the Islamic understanding of Jesus and the Christian faith. In Islam, Jesus is not regarded as the Son of God or as part of a divine trinity. Muslims reject the idea that God has a son or that he came to earth in human form.

Furthermore, Islam teaches that Jesus was not crucified, but that he was instead raised up by God and will return one day. This view is in contrast to the Christian doctrine of Jesus' death on the cross and his resurrection.

Despite these differences, there are also many similarities between the Christian and Islamic understanding of Jesus. Both religions emphasize his moral integrity, his love for God and mankind and his role as a role model for believers, and it is important to note that the understanding of Jesus in Islam is shaped by different theological schools and interpretations. There are also different views on certain aspects of his life and teachings.

CHAPTER 50

Jesus and Judaism

Jesus was a Jewish man who lived in Palestine in the 1st century. He was born into a Jewish family and grew up in a Jewish environment. His teachings and public activities were strongly influenced by Judaism.

Jesus is portrayed in the New Testament of the Bible as a rabbi or teacher who respected Jewish tradition and taught the Torah, the sacred writings of Judaism. He preached on topics such as the Kingdom of God, love of neighbor, forgiveness and the fulfillment of the prophetic scriptures.

Although Jesus was active within Judaism, there were also conflicts between him and some Jewish leaders of his time. Some religious authorities regarded his teachings as controversial or even heretical. This ultimately led to his arrest, trial and crucifixion.

After the death of Jesus, Christianity developed as a separate religion from the Jewish communities. The relationship between Judaism and Christianity has experienced many ups and downs throughout history. There have been times of coexistence and dialog as well as times of conflict and persecution.

It is important to note that the understanding of Jesus varies in Judaism. While some Jewish groups may recognize Jesus as an important teacher, others do not consider him to be the Messiah or Son of God.

In recent decades, however, there has been a growing movement of interfaith dialog between Judaism and Christianity in an attempt to find common ground and promote mutual understanding.

CHAPTER 51

Jesus and the Rosicrucians

The Rosicrucians are an esoteric and mystical movement that originated in Europe in the 17th century. They claim to be based on an ancient secret doctrine allegedly developed by a fictional character named Christian Rosenkreuz. Rosicrucian teachings include topics such as alchemy, Kabbalah, astrology and spiritual transformation.

There are some claims and theories that Jesus himself could have been a member or even the founder of the Rosicrucian movement. This idea is based on the assumption that Jesus could have come into contact with esoteric knowledge during his lost years between his childhood and his public ministry.

It is important to note that there is no historical evidence for these claims and they are not supported by most Christian traditions. The Rosicrucian movement did not emerge until many centuries after the life of Jesus and has its own specific teachings and practices.

It is also worth noting that the idea of Jesus as a member of the Rosicrucian movement is often based on speculative interpretations and conspiracy theories. There are a variety of such theories about the life of Jesus outside of the canonical gospels, but they are considered unfounded or speculative by most theologians and biblical scholars.

Ultimately, the question of a possible connection between Jesus and the Rosicrucians remains open to individual interpretation and belief. However, there is no historical evidence or consensual theological views that would support this connection.

CHAPTER 52

Differences in the Christian faiths

Trinity: The Roman Catholic Church and most Protestant denominations believe in the Trinity, that God exists in three persons - Father, Son (Jesus Christ) and Holy Spirit. However, some non-trinitarian groups such as Jehovah's Witnesses reject the doctrine of the Trinity.

Salvation: There are different views on how people are redeemed. Some denominations emphasize faith in Jesus Christ as the only way to salvation, while others also see good works or sacraments as part of the redemption process.

Church structure:

Roman Catholic Church: It has a hierarchical structure with the Pope as head of the church and bishops who rule over dioceses.

Protestantism: There are different models of church government in Protestantism. For example, Presbyterian churches have elected elders who make decisions together, while Congregationalist churches are led by the members themselves.

Worship and liturgy:

Roman Catholic mass: Mass is a formal liturgical celebration with set prayers, readings from the Bible and sacramental celebrations such as the Eucharist.

Protestant church services: These can vary depending on the denomination, but they often emphasize the sermon and congregational singing. There are fewer formal rites and more freedom in the organization of the service.

Sacraments:

Roman Catholic Church: It recognizes seven sacraments,

including baptism, confirmation, Eucharist, confession, anointing of the sick, marriage and ordination to the priesthood.

Protestantism: The number of sacraments varies depending on the denomination. Some Protestant churches only recognize baptism and communion as sacraments.

Ethics and morals:

Abortion: The Roman Catholic Church rejects abortion as a sin and regards it as the killing of an unborn child. Some Protestant denominations have different views on abortion, with some rejecting it and others allowing certain exceptions.

Homosexuality: Attitudes towards homosexuality vary between Christian denominations. Some reject homosexual relationships as sinful, while others have a more open attitude and accept same-sex marriages or blessings.

These examples are intended to illustrate that there are differences between Christian denominations in various areas of faith. It is important to note that this is not a comprehensive list and that there may be individual variations within each denomination.

CHAPTER 53

Orthodox Church

Theology and teaching:

Divine liturgy: The Orthodox Church emphasizes the importance of the divine liturgy as the central service. It believes that the liturgy is a mystical experience of the presence of God.

Sanctification: The Orthodox Church emphasizes the sanctification or deification of man through the grace of God. This happens through a close relationship with God and the pursuit of holiness.

Church structure:

Patriarchates and autocephaly: The Orthodox Church is divided into various autocephalous (self-governing) churches, which are led by patriarchs or archbishops. Each autocephalous church has its own hierarchy and administration.

Worship and liturgy:

Icon worship: The Orthodox Church has a strong tradition of icon worship, in which icons are seen as windows to the spiritual world.

Liturgical language: In many Orthodox parishes, traditional liturgical languages such as Ancient Greek, Slavonic or Coptic are still used.

Sacraments:

Mystagogy: The Orthodox Church emphasizes the mystagogical nature of the sacraments, in which they are regarded as mysteries that lead the faithful into the presence of God.

Baptism: The Orthodox Church practices baptism by immersion and regards it as the sacrament by which someone is received into the community of believers.

Ethics and morals:

Asceticism: The Orthodox Church emphasizes the importance of asceticism, renunciation and self-control as paths to spiritual maturity and sanctification.

Marriage and divorce: The Orthodox Church has a stricter stance on divorce and recognizes only limited grounds for dissolution of a marriage.

These differences are intended to illustrate that the Orthodox Church has its own theological beliefs, liturgical practices and ethical teachings that distinguish it from other Christian faiths. It is important to note that there can also be regional variations within the Orthodox Church.

World religions and faiths

CHAPTER 54

Gnosis

Gnosticism is a mystical and esoteric movement within Christianity that focuses on the pursuit of spiritual insight and knowledge of the divine nature.

Gnostics often emphasize the duality between spirit and matter as well as salvation through the attainment of spiritual knowledge (gnosis). They often believe in a separation between the material body and the divine spark within each person. Some Gnostic groups also reject the creation of the world by the biblical God and regard him as a lower or false god.

It is important to note that Gnosticism is a very diverse movement and there are many different manifestations. Some Gnostic groups were considered heretical by the early Christian church and their teachings were condemned. Other forms of Gnosticism have developed over time and continue to influence some alternative spiritual traditions today.

CHAPTER 55

New Age Movement

The New Age movement is a spiritual and esoteric movement that emerged in the 1960s and 1970s and has evolved ever since. It encompasses a variety of spiritual practices, belief systems and philosophical approaches that often stem from different religious traditions and esoteric teachings.

The New Age movement often emphasizes personal spiritual development, the pursuit of inner growth and the search for a higher consciousness. Some of the main characteristics of the New Age movement are:

Syncretism: The New Age movement often combines elements from various religious traditions such as Eastern philosophies, indigenous wisdom, esotericism, mysticism and Western esoteric traditions.

Holistic approach: The New Age movement emphasizes the holistic view of the human being, in which body, mind and soul are seen as an inseparable unit. There is a focus on alternative healing methods, energy work, meditation techniques and other practices to promote wellbeing.

Spiritual growth: The New Age movement places great emphasis on personal growth and self-realization. It is often assumed that every person has divine potential and can develop this potential through spiritual practices and insights.

Esoteric teachings: The New Age movement often refers to esoteric teachings and practices such as astrology, tarot, channeling, reincarnation, angel work and crystal healing.

It is important to note that the New Age movement is not

a single organization or set of beliefs. There is great diversity within the movement, and individual beliefs and practices can vary widely. Some people find inspiration and spiritual fulfillment in the New Age movement, while others view it as superficial or incompatible with established religious traditions.

It is also important to note that some traditional religious groups are critical of the New Age movement and reject its teachings as syncretistic or even heretical. As with any spiritual movement, it is advisable to take a critical stance and carefully examine which teachings and practices are right for you personally.

CHAPTER 56

Buddhism and Hinduism

Buddhism and Hinduism are two of the oldest religions in the world and have their origins in India. Although they have some common historical and cultural roots, they differ in their beliefs, practices and teachings.

Hinduism:

Polytheism: Hinduism is a polytheistic religion that believes in the existence of many gods and goddesses. The followers of Hinduism may worship different gods, depending on their personal preference or regional tradition.

Karma and samsara: Hinduism teaches the concept of karma, which states that every action has consequences that affect future lives. The cycle of birth, death and rebirth is known as samsara.

Caste system: Hinduism has a social caste system that divides society into different hierarchies. This system is based on the belief in rebirth and karma.

Vedic scriptures: The sacred scriptures of Hinduism are the Vedas, Upanishads, Bhagavad Gita and other texts. These scriptures contain religious rituals, philosophical discussions and moral teachings.

Buddhism:

No belief in a personal God: Buddhism does not believe in an all-powerful creator God. Instead, Buddhism emphasizes individual responsibility for one's own happiness and suffering.

Four Noble Truths: Buddhism teaches the Four Noble Truths, which describe suffering (dukkha), the causes of suffering, the possibility of ending suffering and the way to end suffering.

Nirvana: The ultimate goal in Buddhism is the attainment of nirvana, a state of liberation from all desires and the endless cycle of birth and death.

Meditation: The practice of meditation plays a central role in Buddhism. The aim of meditation is to heighten awareness, find inner peace and gain insight into the nature of the mind.

It is important to note that both Hinduism and Buddhism are very diverse religions and there are different schools, practices and interpretations within each tradition. These differences can vary depending on geographical region and cultural context.

CHAPTER 57

Taoism

Taoism is a Chinese philosophy and religion based on the concept of the Tao (also Dao). The word "Tao" literally means "way" or "path". Taoism emphasizes the pursuit of harmony with nature and the cosmic principle of the Tao.

Some important aspects of Taoism are:

The Tao: The Tao is often regarded as the immeasurable and indescribable principle that underlies everything. It is the source of all being and the force that guides the universe.

Wu Wei: Wu Wei literally means "do not act" or "do not do". Taoism emphasizes that one should act in accordance with the natural flow of life instead of fighting against it. Wu Wei refers to acting without effort or resistance.

Yin and yang: Yin and yang are two opposing forces or principles that operate in the universe. Yin stands for darkness, femininity and passivity, while yang stands for lightness, masculinity and activity. The aim of Taoism is to achieve a balance between yin and yang.

Meditation and inner alchemy: Taoism emphasizes the practice of meditation to calm the mind and gain insight into the nature of the Tao. There are also techniques of inner alchemy, where one attempts to purify the body and mind and achieve spiritual transformation.

It is important to note that Taoism is a very diverse tradition and encompasses different schools and practices. Some forms of Taoism also have religious aspects with the worship of deities and ancestor worship. Other forms of Taoism are more philosophical.

CHAPTER 58

Judaism

Judaism is one of the oldest monotheistic religions and has its origins in ancient Israel. It is a religion based on the sacred writings of the Tanakh (also known as the Old Testament) and has a rich tradition of laws, customs and beliefs.

Some important aspects of Judaism are:

Monotheism: Judaism believes in a single, all-powerful God who created the universe and rules over everything. This belief in a single God is often referred to as "henotheism", as Judaism also recognizes the existence of other gods, but only worships one God.

Covenant with God: Judaism emphasizes the covenant or contract between God and the Jewish people. According to Jewish tradition, this covenant was made with Abraham and includes certain obligations and commandments that are to be observed by the Jews.

Torah: The Torah is the central holy scripture of Judaism and consists of the five books of Moses (Genesis, Exodus, Leviticus, Numbers and Deuteronomy). It contains religious laws, moral teachings, historical narratives and prophetic messages.

Synagogue: The synagogue is the religious center of the Jewish community. Jews come together there to pray, study the Torah and perform religious rituals together. The rabbi is often the spiritual leader of the community.

Holidays and rituals: Judaism has a large number of holidays and rituals that characterize Jewish religious life. These include, for example, the Sabbath (the weekly day of rest), Passover (the festival of liberation from Egypt), Yom Kippur (the Day of

Atonement) and Hanukkah (the Festival of Lights).

It is important to note that Judaism is a very diverse religion and has different streams and manifestations. There are orthodox, conservative, reformed and other Jewish communities, which can differ in their beliefs, practices and interpretations. Judaism also has a rich cultural tradition with its own music, literature, cuisine and customs.

CHAPTER 59

Islam

Islam is a monotheistic religion that was founded in Arabia in the 7th century by the Prophet Mohammed. Islam is based on the belief in Allah as the one and only God and follows the teachings of the Koran, which is considered the holy book of Islam.

Some important aspects of Islam are:

Monotheism: Islam teaches the belief in a single almighty God, Allah. Muslims believe that Allah is the creator of the universe and rules over everything.

The Prophet Muhammad: Muslims regard Muhammad as the last prophet sent by Allah to proclaim the message of Islam. They see him as a role model for a righteous life and follow his teachings and actions.

The Koran: The Koran is the holy book of Islam and is regarded by Muslims as a direct revelation from Allah to Mohammed. It contains religious commandments, moral teachings, stories and guidelines for daily life.

The Five Pillars of Islam: The Five Pillars are basic religious duties that every Muslim should fulfill. They include the profession of faith (Shahada), ritual prayer (Salat), the alms tax (Zakat), fasting in the month of Ramadan (Sawm) and the pilgrimage to Mecca (Hajj).

Jihad: The word "jihad" literally means "effort" or "endeavor". In Islam, jihad can have different meanings, but in general it refers to a Muslim's effort to live a righteous life and fight against evil. It is often misunderstood and equated with violent action, although the majority of jihad is understood as an inner struggle for self-improvement.

It is important to note that Islam is a very diverse religion and has different currents and manifestations. There are Sunni, Shia and other Muslim communities, which can differ in their beliefs, practices and interpretations. Islam also has a rich cultural tradition with its own art, architecture, music and customs.

CHAPTER 60

Freemasonry

Freemasonry is an international brotherhood or secret society based on moral and ethical principles. It has its roots in the 17th and 18th centuries in Europe and has since spread worldwide.

Freemasonry emphasizes the ideals of tolerance, brotherhood, equality and personal development. The members are called Freemasons and meet in so-called lodges to perform ritual ceremonies, discuss moral teachings and undertake social activities.

Freemasonry is known for its symbolic language and rituals, which are often based on building and craft metaphors. It uses symbols such as the protractor, the compass or the temple building to convey moral and philosophical teachings.

There are various Masonic orders or grand lodges around the world, each of which has its own traditions and rituals. Membership in Freemasonry is usually male, but there are also some mixed or all-female lodges.

In most grand lodges, the belief in a higher being called the Master Builder is considered the smallest common creed, and Freemasonry has caused much controversy throughout history and has often been associated with conspiracy theories. It is important to note that most Masonic activities are based on social gatherings, humanitarian projects and personal development, and since Freemasonry is a secret society, not all information about its rituals and practices is publicly available. If you would like to learn more about Freemasonry, I recommend contacting a local lodge or Masonic order for more information.

CHAPTER 61

Shamanism

The oldest known religion is shamanism, which was practiced thousands of years ago. Shamanism is a spiritual practice based on the belief in spirits and communication with them. There is archaeological evidence that shamanistic practices existed in Europe and Asia as early as 40,000 to 50,000 years ago.

However, it is important to note that it is difficult to pinpoint an exact dating of the oldest religion, as religious beliefs and practices were often passed down orally and did not leave written records. There are also different regional and cultural variations of shamanism, as well as other early religious traditions such as animism, which can also be considered some of the oldest religions.

It is also possible that there were even older religious beliefs of which we have no knowledge, as they have not been documented by archaeological finds or other sources. The question of the oldest religion therefore remains a subject of research and discussion.

CHAPTER 62

The importance of religion and faith for humanity

Creating meaning: Religion and faith offer many people a framework for understanding the meaning of life and finding answers to fundamental questions about the origin, purpose and destiny of human beings. They offer a meta-narrative that goes beyond the purely material and can help people to understand their existence in a wider context.

Comfort and hope: In difficult times, faith can give people comfort, support and hope. Belief in a higher power or a spiritual concept can help people deal with grief, loss or other challenges. The thought of divine care or an afterlife can comfort people and give them hope.

Community and cohesion: Religions often create communities of believers who support each other, strengthen social ties and share common values. Religious institutions such as churches, mosques or temples offer places of gathering and exchange. Religious rituals and celebrations can also promote cohesion within a community.

Ethics and moral guidance: Religions often provide ethical guidelines and moral principles that can help believers distinguish between right and wrong and guide their behavior accordingly. Religious teachings can serve as a basis for moral decisions and help people to lead a meaningful and virtuous life.

Identity and cultural heritage: Religion plays an important role in the formation of individual identities and the preservation of cultural traditions and customs. Religious practices, rituals and beliefs can be part of a person's personal identity and give them a sense of belonging to a particular community or culture. Religion can also serve as a link between generations by passing on cultural heritage.

Inspiration and creative expression: Religion often has a strong influence on art, music, literature and other forms of creative expression. Religious stories, symbols and ideas can serve as a source of inspiration and encourage artists to express their spiritual experiences in their art.

It is important to note that the impact of religion and belief on humanity can be both positive and negative. While they offer comfort, hope and guidance to many people, they can also lead to conflict, prejudice and discrimination. The impact of religion and belief often depends on the way it is practiced and interpreted. It is important that religious beliefs are practiced with respect for the diversity of other faiths and worldviews.

CHAPTER 63

What significance does God have for humanity?

Existential meaning: The question of God concerns fundamental questions of human existence, such as the origin and purpose of life, the nature of the universe and human identity. It touches on the deepest existential needs and longings of human beings.

Meaning Foundation: Belief in God can help people find meaning in their lives. It provides a meta-narrative that goes beyond the purely material and helps people understand their existence in a larger context. Belief in God can give life meaning and purpose.

Comfort and hope: Faith in God can give people comfort, support and hope in difficult times. The idea of a higher power or a divine plan can help people to deal with grief, loss or other challenges. The thought of divine care or life after death can give comfort and hope.

Ethics and moral guidance: Belief in God can serve as a basis for ethical guidelines and help people to distinguish between right and wrong. Religious teachings can serve as a source of inspiration to lead a meaningful and virtuous life.

Community and cohesion: Religions often create communities of believers who support each other, strengthen social ties and share common values. Belief in God can bring people together and promote cohesion within a community.

It is important to note that the question of God can have different meanings for different people. Not everyone asks this question or finds it an important source of meaning. The meaning of God and religion is strongly influenced by individual beliefs, cultural backgrounds and personal experiences.

CHAPTER 64

The meaning of life

The question of the meaning of life is a fundamental and complex question that can be viewed from different philosophical, religious and personal perspectives. There is no single answer to this question, as the meaning of life depends on individual beliefs, values and experiences. However, here are some possible aspects:

Self-actualization: Some people believe that the meaning of life is to develop one's potential and realize oneself. This can mean achieving personal goals, developing talents or making a contribution to society.

Relationships and love: For many people, the meaning of life lies in interpersonal relationships and love for other people. Maintaining friendships, family ties and romantic partnerships can be seen as a central aspect of a meaningful life.

Service to others: The belief in helping others and having a positive impact on the world can be seen as the meaning of life. This can be achieved through volunteer work, professional activities or social commitment.

Spiritual search: For many people, the meaning of life lies in a spiritual search for transcendence or a connection with a higher power or a greater whole. Religions often provide a framework for this search for spiritual fulfillment.

Meaning through creativity: Some people find the meaning of life in creative forms of expression such as art, music or literature. The creation of something new and the opportunity to express oneself through creative activities can be perceived as meaningful.

It is important to note that the meaning of life is an individual question and each person can find their own meaning. What is meaningful for one person may not be for another. There is no universal answer to this question; it is up to each individual to discover and define their own meaning.

CHAPTER 65

Life after death

The question of life after death is one of the most fundamental and at the same time most puzzling questions that mankind has always grappled with. There are different views and beliefs on this subject:

Religious beliefs: Many religions believe in life after death. However, the exact ideas vary depending on the religion. Christianity, for example, believes in a resurrection of the body and eternal life in heaven or hell. Hinduism and Buddhism believe in rebirth or reincarnation, in which the soul is reborn in a new body.

Spiritual beliefs: Some people have spiritual beliefs that believe in a continuation of the soul or consciousness after death. These beliefs can range from an existence in another dimension to a union with a universal energy.

Atheistic view: Atheists reject the belief in life after death and regard death as the final end of consciousness and individual existence.

It is important to note that there is no scientific evidence for life after death, as it is a metaphysical question that lies outside the realm of empirical research. Belief in life after death is often based on personal convictions, religious teachings or spiritual experiences.

Ultimately, the question of life after death remains an individual and subjective question that each person must answer for themselves. It is important that everyone respects their own convictions and remains open to the diversity of views on this topic.

CHAPTER 66

The Omega Point

The term "Omega Point" was coined by the French Jesuit priest and philosopher Pierre Teilhard de Chardin. He used it to describe a hypothetical state of evolution in which the entire universe reaches a climax or a higher form of consciousness.

Teilhard de Chardin believed that evolution is a purposeful process working towards ever greater complexity and consciousness. The Omega Point represents the end point of this evolutionary process, where the entire universe is united in a state of perfect unity and consciousness.

According to Teilhard de Chardin, the Omega Point would represent a kind of cosmic consciousness in which all individual consciousnesses merge and become a higher form of being. This state would mean a complete union with God or a transcendent reality.

It is important to note that the Omega Point is criticized by many scientists and philosophers as it is considered speculative and not based on science. It is a metaphysical idea based on religious and philosophical beliefs.

The Omega Point therefore remains a concept that was developed by Teilhard de Chardin and is discussed in more detail in his work "The Phenomenon of Man". However, it is not generally accepted or widely used in scientific or philosophical circles.

CHAPTER 67

Parallel universes

The idea of parallel universes, also known as the multiverse, is a concept from theoretical physics and cosmology. It states that, in addition to our known universe, there may be other universes that exist parallel to ours.

There are various theories and models that postulate the existence of parallel universes. One of these is the so-called "many worlds interpretation" of quantum mechanics, which states that for every quantum mechanical measurement, all possible outcomes occur simultaneously and manifest themselves in different parallel universes. A different version of reality would exist in each of these universes.

Another theory is the "inflation theory" in the context of cosmological modeling. It states that our universe was created during an extremely rapid expansion phase and that bubbles could have formed in the process. Each of these bubbles could represent a separate universe that exists parallel to ours.

It is important to note that the existence of parallel universes has not yet been empirically proven and is therefore still the subject of scientific discussion and research. The idea of parallel universes remains speculative and hypothetical for the time being.

There are also philosophical considerations about parallel universes, particularly in relation to questions about the existence of other life forms or the possibility of alternative choices and trajectories in other universes. However, these considerations are speculative and cannot be answered by scientific methods.

Overall, the concept of parallel universes remains a fascinating topic that continues to be researched and discussed, both in physics and in philosophy.

CHAPTER 68

Akasha

Akasha is a term used in Indian philosophy and spirituality, particularly in Hinduism and Buddhism. It refers to the cosmic or universal consciousness, which is regarded as an all-encompassing energy field in which all information and experiences of the universe are stored.

The term "Akasha" comes from Sanskrit and literally means "ether" or "space". It is often described as a kind of etheric medium that forms the basis for all material phenomena. Akasha is also regarded as the fifth element alongside earth, water, fire and air.

In the concept of Akasha, all thoughts, feelings, actions and events of past, present and future times are stored. It is believed that spiritual practitioners can access this universal consciousness through meditation or other techniques to gain information or insight.

It is important to note that the concept of Akasha is rather metaphysical and cannot be proven by scientific methods. It is a spiritual concept rooted in the religious and philosophical traditions of India.

Overall, Akasha remains a concept used in Indian philosophy and spirituality to describe the all-encompassing consciousness or energy field in which all the information of the universe is stored. However, it is important to note that there are different interpretations and conceptions of Akasha, depending on religious or philosophical tradition.

Closing words

In the depths of our faith, we find what drives us. Faith in something greater than ourselves gives us hope and fills our hearts with love. But it is charity that makes us true creators.

We are creatures of the universe, but the miracle of creation lies in our children. They are our greatest gift in our earthly existence. Through them, we experience unconditional love and learn that we have a responsibility as parents and mentors.

Let us fill their hearts with faith so that they can realize their dreams. Let us give them love so that they can grow up in a world full of compassion. Let us give them hope so that they never lose heart.

Through our children, we have become creators. We can shape and form the world around us. We can build bridges and overcome boundaries. We can help each other and grow together.

May we always be reminded that faith, love, hope and charity are the cornerstones of our existence. May we carry these values in our hearts and strive for them in every moment of our lives.

May they become creators in their own journey and illuminate the world with their light.

Together, let us lead humanity into a future in which faith, love, hope and charity are the basis for a fulfilled and harmonious life.

In gratitude for the miracle of life and the opportunity to become a creature and a creator.

From the bottom of my heart, I would like to thank my parents for giving me the precious gift of life. Their love and care have made me the person I am today.

I would also like to thank my wife from the bottom of my heart for giving me the greatest gift of my life. Through her love and devotion, I became the proud father of our child. It is a blessing to be able to share this wonderful gift with her.

Printed in Great Britain
by Amazon